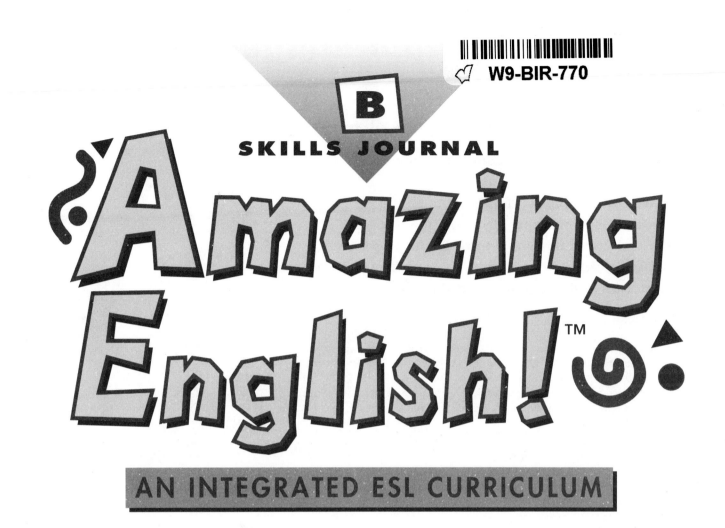

B

SKILLS JOURNAL

¡Amazing English!™

AN INTEGRATED ESL CURRICULUM

Addison-Wesley Publishing Company

A Publication of the World Language Division

Director of Product Development: Judith M. Bittinger
Executive Editor: Elinor Chamas
Content Development: Elly Schottman, Susan Hooper
Editorial Development: Elly Schottman
Text and Cover Design: Taurins Design Associates
Art Direction and Production: Taurins Design Associates
Production and Manufacturing: James W. Gibbons

Illustrators: Teresa Anderko 70; Ellen Appleby 61, 86; Dolores Bego 99; Lee Lee Brazeal 6, 48, 49, 50, 56; Mena Dolobowsky 18, 41, 82, 83, 94, 108; Joanna Fabris 31; Meryl Henderson 20, 101; Steve Henry 4, 36; Pat Hoggan 10, 13, 85, 87, 89; Gay Holland 42, 80, 84, 96; Linda Knox 58, 64, 98; Steve Mach 15, 24, 25, 30, 33, 40, 44, 53, 71, 91, 103, 105; Ben Mahan 1, 45, 100; Susan Miller 2, 8, 23, 37, 76, 95; Diane Paterson 46, 60, 65, 78, 97; Deborah Pinkney 9, 22; Chris Reed 51; John Sandford 63, 68, 69; Jackie Snider 21, 47, 75, 90.

ISBN 0-201-85368-X
3 4 5 6 7 8 9 10-CRS-99 98 97

CONTENTS

Read and follow directions.

1. Color the school bus yellow.

2. Draw a clock on the wall.

3. Color the chair blue.

4. Draw a book on the table.

5. Draw a boy next to the desk.

6. Color the chalkboard green.

SCHOOL

(Supports Language Activities Big Book B, Activity 1) **Following directions; reviewing key vocabulary.**
Review names of school objects by asking volunteers to name things they see in the picture. Have their classmates point to the items they name. Read the directions together. Students can then work in pairs to complete the page.

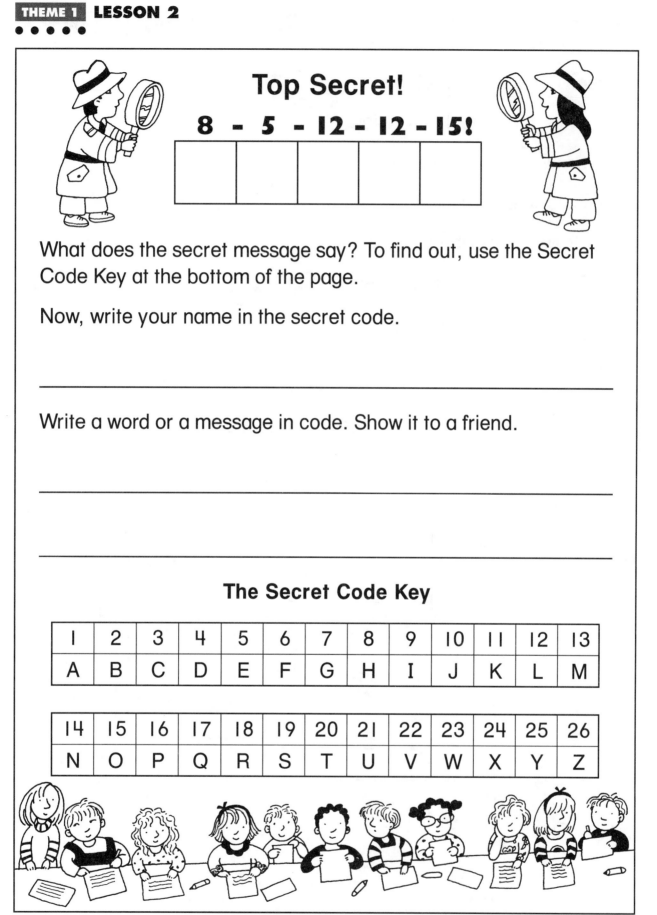

Top Secret!

8 - 5 - 12 - 12 - 15!

What does the secret message say? To find out, use the Secret Code Key at the bottom of the page.

Now, write your name in the secret code.

_____

Write a word or a message in code. Show it to a friend.

_____

_____

The Secret Code Key

1	2	3	4	5	6	7	8	9	10	11	12	13
A	B	C	D	E	F	G	H	I	J	K	L	M

14	15	16	17	18	19	20	21	22	23	24	25	26
N	O	P	Q	R	S	T	U	V	W	X	Y	Z

(Supports Student Book B, page 3) **Using secret codes; reviewing number words.** Help students use the Secret Code Key to decode the word (HELLO) at the top of this page. Write several words in code on the board, for more group decoding practice, then have students complete the page independently. To practice number words, ask students to copy their name in code on a strip of paper. Collect the papers. Have a student choose a strip and read the numbers aloud. Students write down the numbers, and decode the name.

My name is _____.

I am in _____ grade.

Check (✔) one:

     ____ I come to school by bus.

     ____ I come to school by car.

     ____ I walk to school.

Draw a picture of yourself
or glue your photo here.

My teacher's name is_____

Here are the names of some kids in my class:

_____,_____

_____,_____

At school, I like _____

_____

(Supports Student Book B, pages 4-7) **Writing a journal entry.** Preview this page with the class. Read each sentence starter aloud and allow students to give sample answers. Encourage students to brainstorm lots of different responses to the last sentence starter. You may want to list ideas from this discussion on the board. This will provide optional support for students as they complete the page independently. You may want to save this page in the student's **Assessment Portfolio.**

3

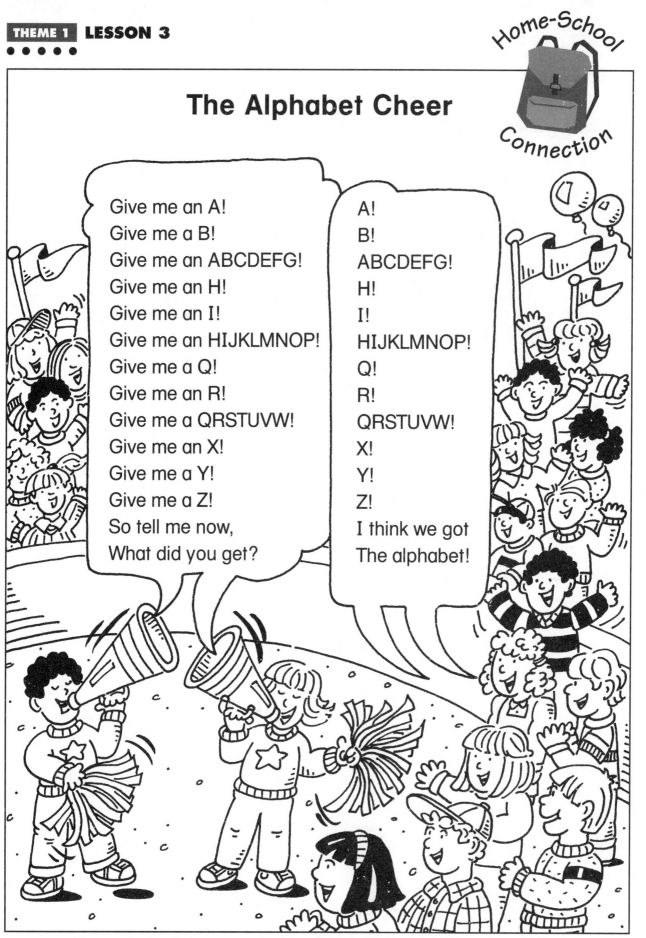

The Alphabet Cheer

Give me an A!
Give me a B!
Give me an ABCDEFG!
Give me an H!
Give me an I!
Give me an HIJKLMNOP!
Give me a Q!
Give me an R!
Give me a QRSTUVW!
Give me an X!
Give me a Y!
Give me a Z!
So tell me now,
What did you get?

A!
B!
ABCDEFG!
H!
I!
HIJKLMNOP!
Q!
R!
QRSTUVW!
X!
Y!
Z!
I think we got
The alphabet!

(Supports Student Book B, pages 4-7) **Home-School Connection.** Review "The Alphabet Cheer." It is recorded on the audio tape for Theme 1, Lesson 1 (LABB 1). Have the class perform it as a two-part chant. Encourage student pairs to practice reading the cheer aloud together. Have students take this page home and share "The Alphabet Cheer" with their families.

What time is it?

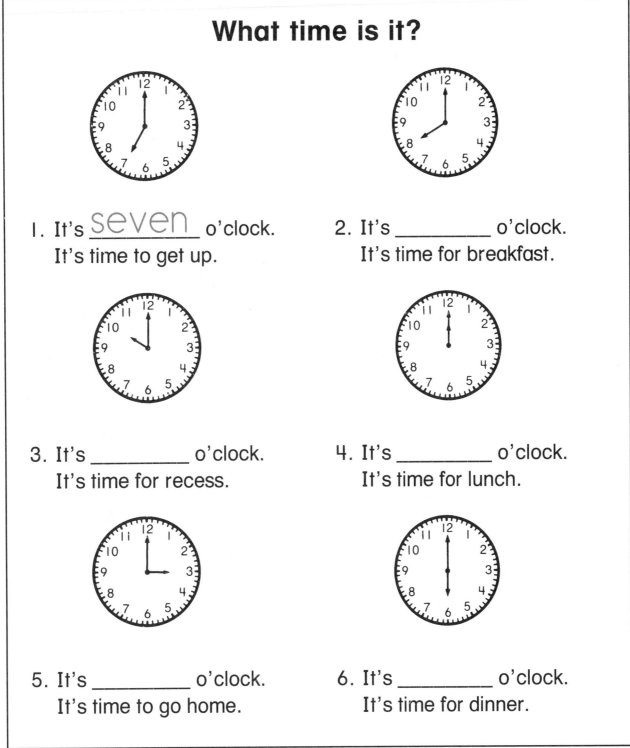

1. It's ___seven___ o'clock.
   It's time to get up.

2. It's _____ o'clock.
   It's time for breakfast.

3. It's _____ o'clock.
   It's time for recess.

4. It's _____ o'clock.
   It's time for lunch.

5. It's _____ o'clock.
   It's time to go home.

6. It's _____ o'clock.
   It's time for dinner.

(Supports Language Activities Big Book B, Activity 2) **Telling time on the hour; reviewing number words.** Play a spelling game to review number words *one - twelve*. Draw a line for each letter of a word. Students must discover the word by guessing the letters. When a correct letter is named, write it on the line. Be sure to include number words *three, six, seven, eight, ten,* and *twelve* in this game. Leave the words on the board for spelling assistance. Discuss this page thoroughly with the class, then have students write the answers independently.

Find the word that matches each picture.
Glue the word in the box.

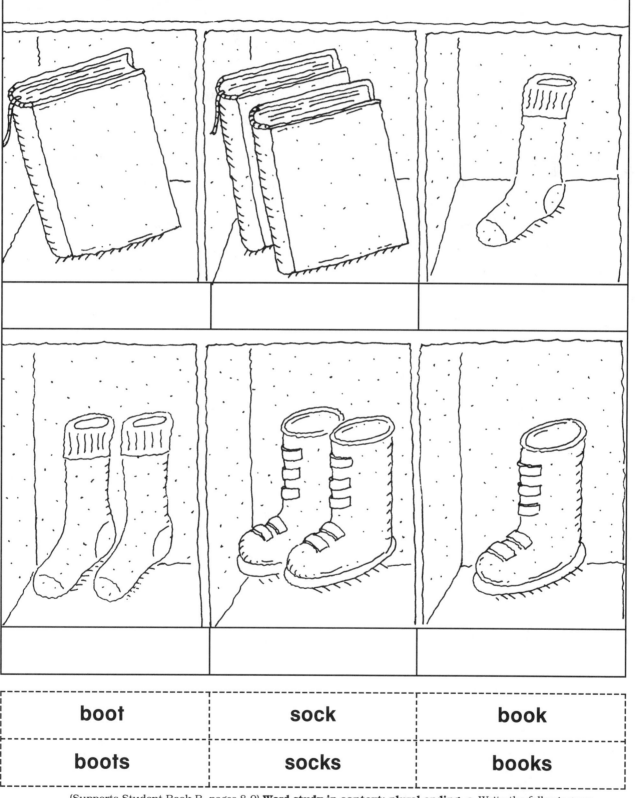

boot	sock	book
boots	socks	books

© Addison-Wesley Publishing Company

(Supports Student Book B, pages 8-9) **Word study in context: plural ending -s.** Write the following sentences on the board: *I walk to school with my friends. I carry my books and my lunch.* Ask volunteers to underline and read the words that end with the letter *s*. Discuss the generalization that an *-s* added to the end of a noun shows that there is more than one. Read the word pairs at the bottom of this page together and discuss the items shown in the picture. Have students cut out the word cards and glue them in the appropriate boxes.

My Friend

This is my friend, _____.

_____ is very _____.

We like to _____

_____.

(Supports Student Book B, page 10) **Writing a journal entry.** Ask students to think of someone who is their friend. It may be a child or an adult; it may be a family member. Students will draw a picture at the top of this page. Read each sentence starter aloud and encourage students to give sample answers. You may want to list the adjectives and activities they suggest on the board for support as students complete this page independently. You may want to save this page in the student's **Assessment Portfolio**.

A B C D E F G H I J K L M N O P Q R S T U V W X Y Z

Ask six friends to write their names here.

_____   _____

_____   _____

_____   _____

Now write their names in alphabetical order.

1. _____

2. _____

3. _____

4. _____

5. _____

6. _____

(Supports Student Book B, page 11) **Gathering data; alphabetizing.** Review the skill of alphabetizing by asking each child to write his or her name on a piece of paper. Divide the class into several groups. Have each
group in turn come to the front of the class and line themselves up in alphabetical order. Provide instruction
and help as needed. Ask the rest of the class to check for correctness. Review the directions on this page, then
have students do the activity.

8

Find the matching picture.

_____ 1. I want to ride my bike. _____ 2. I want to play ball.

_____ 3. I want to jump rope. _____ 4. I want to draw.

_____ 5. I want to read. _____ 6. I want to roller-skate.

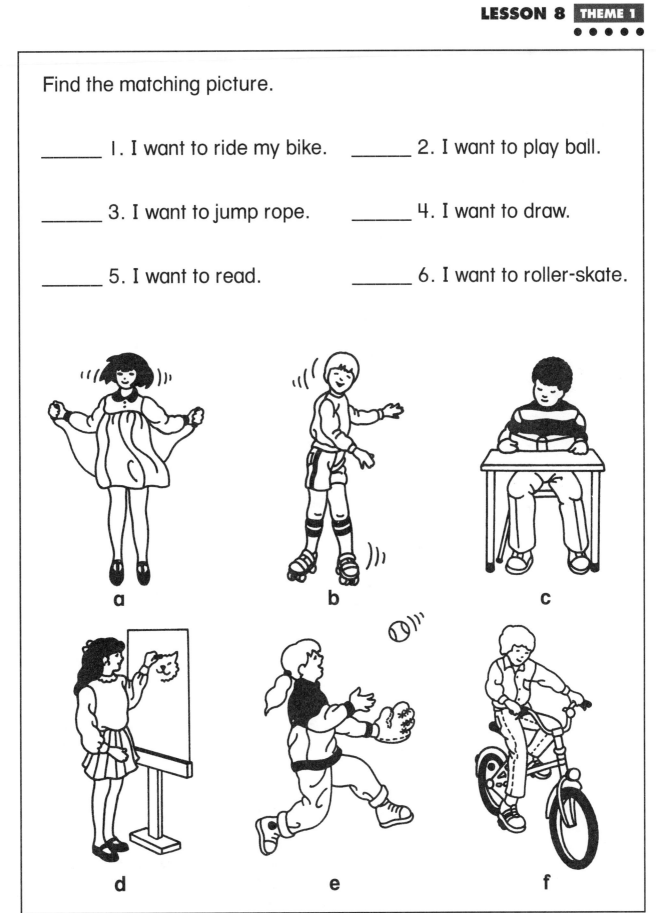

a

b

c

d

e

f

(Supports Language Activities Big Book B, Activity 3) **Reinforcing language structure: _I want to...;_ matching sentences with pictures**. Students read each sentence, find the matching picture, and write the letter of the picture on the line. Some students will be able to complete this page independently, others may need assistance.

The Rabbit and the Turnip

Rabbit takes the turnip to Donkey's house.
What happens next?
Draw a map of the story.
Draw the homes of the animals.
Show where each animal takes the turnip.
Then show how the story ends.

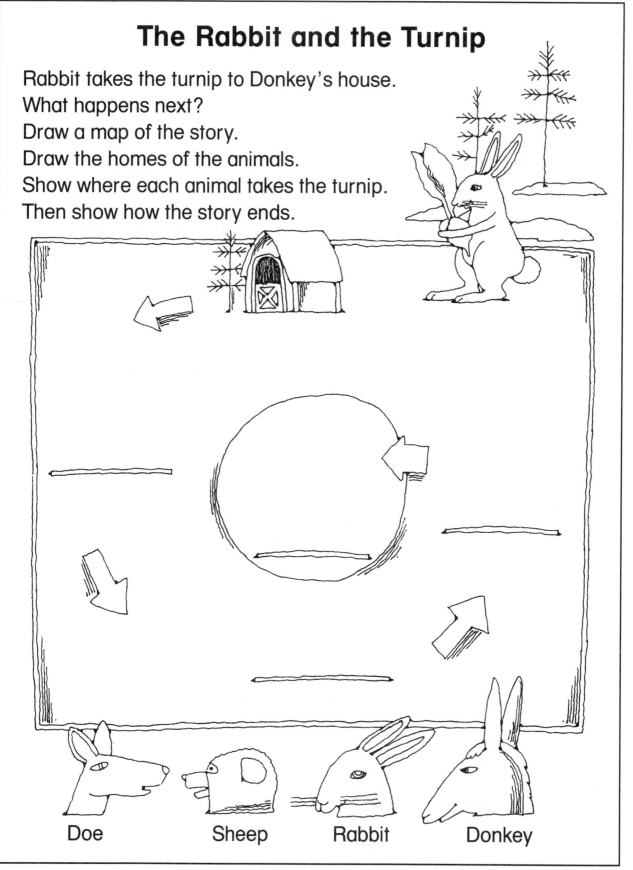

Doe   Sheep   Rabbit   Donkey

10

(Supports Big Book: *The Rabbit and the Turnip*) **Sequencing, creating a story map, retelling a story.** Read the directions aloud. Help students recall the events of *The Rabbit and the Turnip* and clarify the directions as you point to the story map and ask: *Where did Rabbit take the turnip? Where did Donkey take the turnip?* (to Sheep's house) *What will you draw here?* (Sheep's house) *What will you write on the line?* (Sheep) *Where did Sheep take the turnip?* etc. Have students use their completed story map to retell the story.

Toss a penny.

Heads 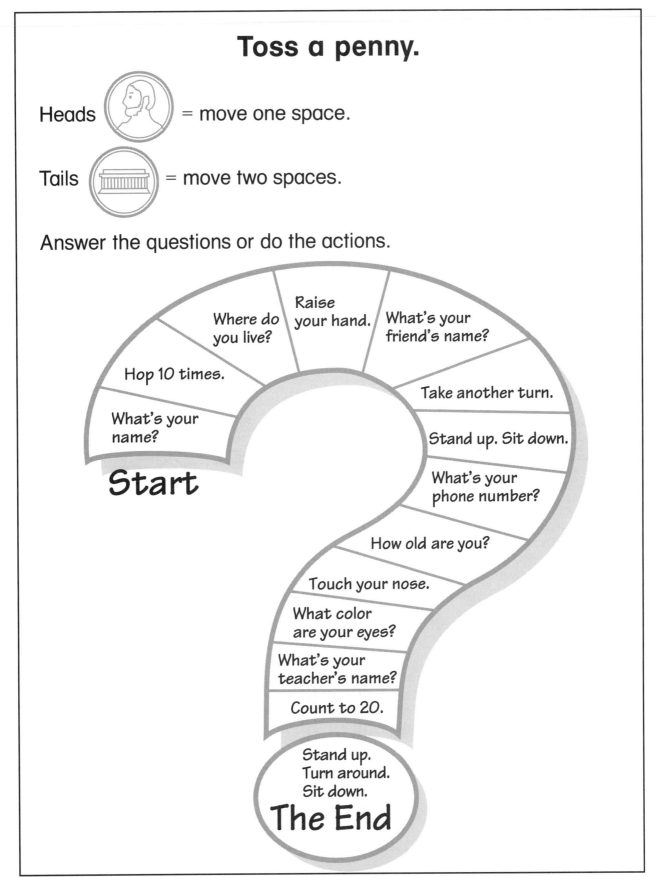 = move one space.

Tails = move two spaces.

Answer the questions or do the actions.

Where do you live?

Raise your hand.

What's your friend's name?

Hop 10 times.

Take another turn.

What's your name?

Stand up. Sit down.

Start

What's your phone number?

How old are you?

Touch your nose.

What color are your eyes?

What's your teacher's name?

Count to 20.

Stand up. Turn around. Sit down.

The End

(Supports Language Activities Big Book B, Activity 4) **Providing information about self; following written directions.** Students will play this game in small groups. Each group will use one game board and one penny. Each player will need a small game marker. It may be best for students to sit on the floor to play this game. Review the instructions and the sentences on the game board. Demonstrate how the game is played. After playing the game with classmates, students can take this game board home to share with their families.

11

What can you do?

Circle **I can** or **I can't.**

1. I can

       ride a bike.

   I can't

2. I can

       play the piano.

   I can't

3. I can

       ice skate.

   I can't

4. I can

       ride a horse.

   I can't

5. I can

       play soccer.

   I can't

6. I can

       swim.

   I can't

Finish the sentences any way you like.
Draw a picture.

I can _____.

I can't _____.

(Supports Language Activities Big Book B, Activity 5) **Answering a questionnaire; providing information about self.** Students read each sentence and circle *I can* or *I can't* according to their own abilities. Then they draw a picture of something they <u>can</u> do and a picture of something they <u>can not</u> do. They complete the sentences below the pictures. Provide help as needed. Allow time for volunteers to read their sentences aloud.

Thank You, Little Doe!

Little Rabbit shared his turnip with his friend Little Donkey.
Little Donkey gave the turnip to Little Doe.
Little Doe gave the turnip to Little Rabbit.
Little Rabbit gobbled it right up!

Help Little Rabbit write a thank-you letter to Little Doe.

Dear Little Doe,

_____

_____

_____

_____

Your friend,
Little Rabbit

(Supports Big Book: *The Rabbit and the Turnip*) **Writing a friendly letter; extending story ideas; creating a story sequel.** Review the directions aloud. Have students brainstorm ideas for the thank-you letter. Encourage lots of different suggestions. You may want to write these ideas on the board. This will provide optional support for students as they complete this page independently. You may want to save this page in the student's **Assessment Portfolio**.

Write your initials next to your birthday month.
Ask a friend, "When is your birthday?"
Ask five friends to write their initials next to their
birthday months.

Take this graph home. Ask people in your family
to write their initials on the birthday graph.

	1	2	3	4	5	6	7	8	9	10
January										
February										
March										
April										
May										
June										
July										
August										
September										
October										
November										
December										

(Supports Student Book B, page 16) **Graphing and analyzing data; Home-School Connection.** Read directions aloud. Use an extra copy of this graph to demonstrate how to gather and record information: *When is your birthday? Write your initials here, please.* Have students practice the language and the procedure, then have them complete the classroom portion of the survey. Ask students to bring the graph back to class after surveying their family. Discuss and compile the results. *Which month has the most/the fewest birthdays?*

clock	play ball	bus	friends
read	ride a bike	school	sneakers
jump rope	soup	books	window
skate	knapsack	lunch box	socks

Reinforcing key vocabulary. Have students cut out the cards and match pictures with words. Students can use the set of cards (16 picture cards and 16 word cards) to play a game of Concentration alone or with a partner. As a variation, two students may combine their picture cards, or their word cards and lay out a Concentration game in which they will hunt for picture or word pairs. The picture and word cards on this page will also be used with the Amazing Words game board on page 17.

AMAZING WORDS

Put nine pictures on the game board.
Play an Amazing Words game.

Reinforcing key vocabulary. Each student chooses nine **picture cards** (provided on page 15) to glue on the game board. Two or three students play *Amazing Words* together. Players combine their sets of **word cards** from page 15 and place them face down on a table. In turn, each player picks up a word card and reads it aloud. If the matching picture appears on that player's game board, he or she places the word card on top of the picture. If not, the word card is returned to the table. The first player to fill his or her game board wins.

Draw furniture in a room.
Write the word by each piece of furniture.

This is a __ bedroom __ bathroom __ kitchen __ living room

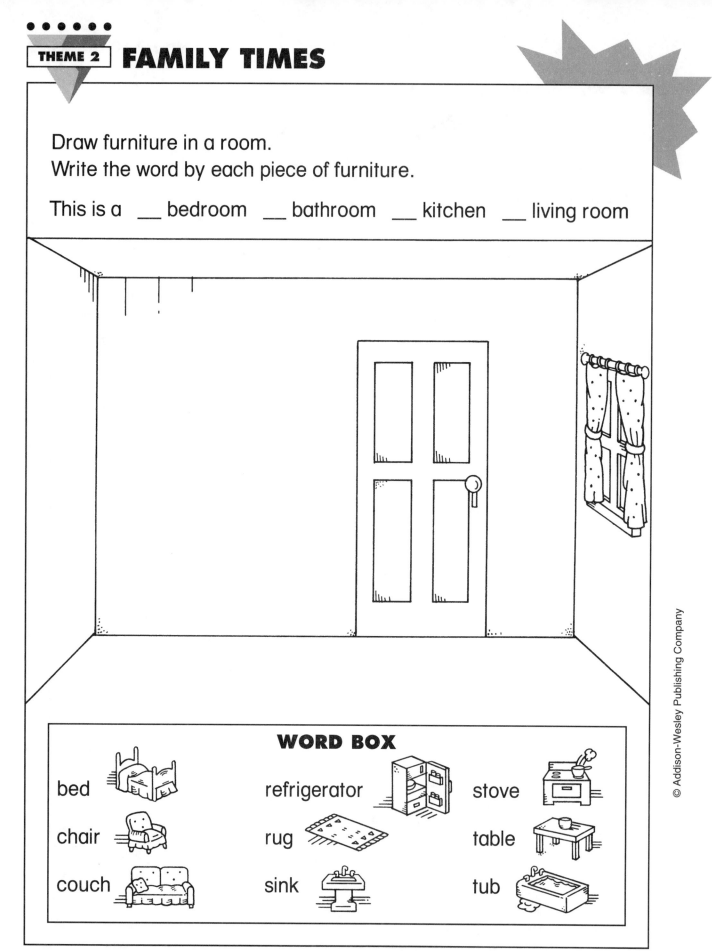

WORD BOX

bed

refrigerator

stove

chair

rug

table

couch

sink

tub

(Supports Language Activities Big Book B, Activity 7) **Drawing and labeling a diagram; reinforcing key vocabulary.** Read the directions aloud. Each student will choose to draw a bedroom, a bathroom, a kitchen, or a living room. Have students place a check in front of the name of the room that they will draw. Direct attention to the Word Box. Ask, *What furniture would you draw in a (bedroom)?* After adequate discussion, have students complete the page independently.

Home-School
Connection

I love you in the morning
And in the afternoon.
I love you in the evening,
Underneath the moon.

Skidamarink a dink, a dink
Skidamarink a doo.
I love you!

Draw pictures of yourself and someone you love.
What do the two of you do in the morning?
What do you do in the afternoon?
Write a sentence to go with each picture.

In the morning

_____

_____

_____

In the afternoon

_____

_____

_____

(Supports Student Book B, page 15) **Home-School Connection.** Sing the song "Skidamarink." Have students track the words as they sing. Ask students to think of someone (or something) they love. What do they like to do with that person, animal, or toy in the morning? What do they like to do together in the afternoon? Encourage students to share their ideas in a discussion, then circulate as they independently complete the page. Students can take this page home and share the song and their work with their families.

Find the matching picture.
Write the missing word.

___c___ 1. My ___little brother___ is sleeping.

_____ 2. My _____ _____ is taking a shower.

_____ 3. My _____ are getting dressed.

_____ 4. My _____ _____ is eating.

_____ 5. My _____ _____ is packing my lunch.

a

b

c

d

e

© Addison-Wesley Publishing Company

(Supports Language Activities Big Book B, Activity 8) **Reinforcing key vocabulary; matching sentences to pictures.** Direct attention to the pictures on this page. Explain to students that in this family, there are two parents, a big brother, a little brother, a big sister, and a little sister. Point to each picture and ask: *Who is this?* Direct attention to the top of the page. Students will match each sentence with the correct picture. They will write the letter of the picture on the line, then complete the sentence with the correct word(s).

20

Write the missing words in the crossword puzzle.

1. ⇨ My _____ came back

2. ⇨ _____ old Japan

2. ⬇ And brought with her a lovely _____.

3. ⬇ My aunt _____ back

4. ⬇ From _____

5. ⇨ And brought with _____

6. ⇨ A fine _____.

Finish this verse any way you like. Can you make it rhyme? The pictures will give you some ideas.

My aunt came back
From old Turkey
And brought with her

_____

key   monkey   bee   donkey   tree   tea

(Supports Student Book B, pages 16-17) **Reinforcing key vocabulary, creating an original song verse.** Students can refer to the text of "My Aunt Came Back" as they write the missing words in the puzzle. Have students suggest lots of different endings for the new song verse. Encourage them to add an adjective to give their line the right number of beats. (... an old donkey, a shiny key, etc.) Each student will write down his or her favorite final line.

Look at the picture.
Answer the questions.

1. How many brothers does she have?

   She has _____.

2. How many cats does she have?

   She has _____.

3. How many dogs does she have?

   She has _____.

My Family
Draw a picture of your family.
Then write about your family.

My Family

I have _____

_____

(Supports Language Activities Big Book B, Activity 9) **Following oral instructions; getting information from pictures; providing information about self.** Give students directions for coloring the picture. *Color one dog red. Color one dog yellow. Color two cats gray. Color one cat brown.* Students answer the questions about the picture. Then they draw a picture of their own family and write a sentence about their own family members and pets.

22

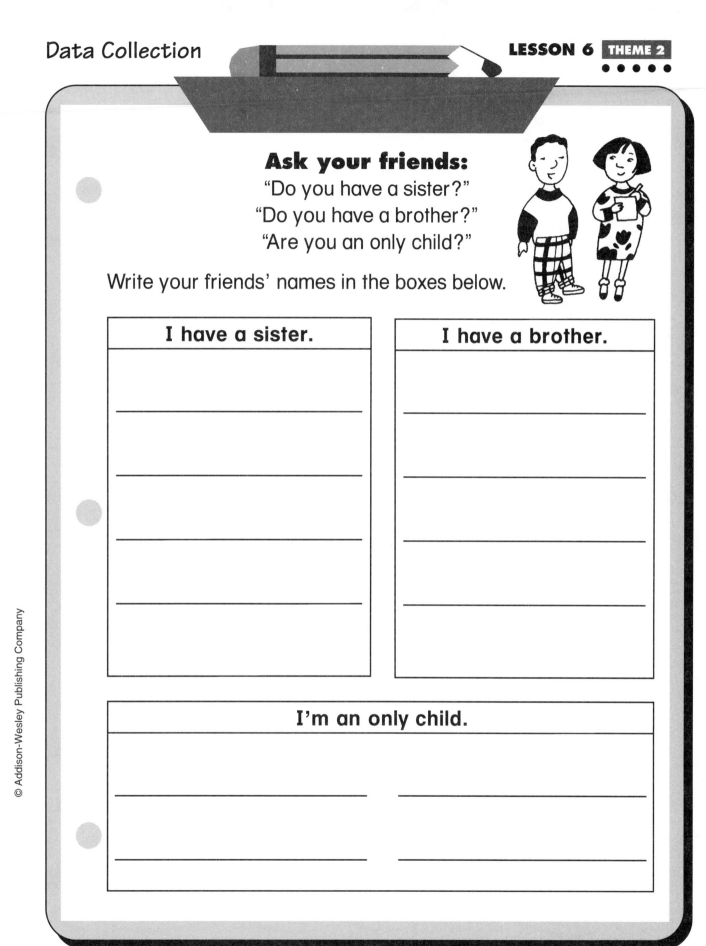

Ask your friends:

"Do you have a sister?"

"Do you have a brother?"

"Are you an only child?"

Write your friends' names in the boxes below.

I have a sister.

I have a brother.

I'm an only child.

(Supports Language Activities Big Book B, Activity 10) **Taking a survey, analyzing data.** Give students a set amount of time in which to conduct the survey. Then, have students discuss their data. Ask questions: *Which box had the most /the fewest names? Did everyone get the same result? Why do you think so? Did you write anyone's name in two boxes? Did you write anyone's name in all three boxes? Why not? If you did this survey with everyone in the world, which box do you think would have the most / the least names?*

What do you like to do with your family?

I like to watch TV with my family.　　YES　NO

I like to go on trips with my family.　　YES　NO

I like to go shopping with my family.　　YES　NO

I like to play games with my family.　　YES　NO

Write a story about something you like to do with someone in your family. Draw a picture, too.

My _____ and I like to _____

_____

_____

_____

© Addison-Wesley Publishing Company

(Supports Student Book B, pages 18-20) **Answering a questionnaire, writing a journal entry.** Preview the page with the students. Students answer the questionnaire at the top of the page by filling in the box marked *Yes* or *No*. Then they write and illustrate a story about something they like to do with someone in their family. You may want to save this page in the student's **Assessment Portfolio**.

1. This is Ana. What is she doing?

_____

2. This is Tony. What is he doing?

_____

3. This is Ana, Tony, and their mother.
What are they doing?

_____

Draw a picture of yourself.
What are you doing?

I am _____

(Supports Language Activities Big Book B, Activity 11) **Writing sentences; reinforcing key language.** Point
to the first item on this page and have students read the sentences and answer the question aloud: *She is
tying her shoe.* Write the answer on the board and draw attention to the capital letter at the beginning of the
sentence and the period at the end. Discuss the other two pictures, then have students complete the page
independently. You may want to save this page in the student's **Assessment Portfolio**.

Read the sentences.
Write the missing word.

me   you   him   her   us   them

1. I am making lemonade.

   Can you help _____?

2. Bill is fixing his bike.

   Can you help _____?

3. Jill is making cookies.

   Can you help _____?

4. They are washing their dog.

   Can you help _____?

5. You are feeding the dog.

   Can I help _____?

6. We are making juice.

   Can you help _____?

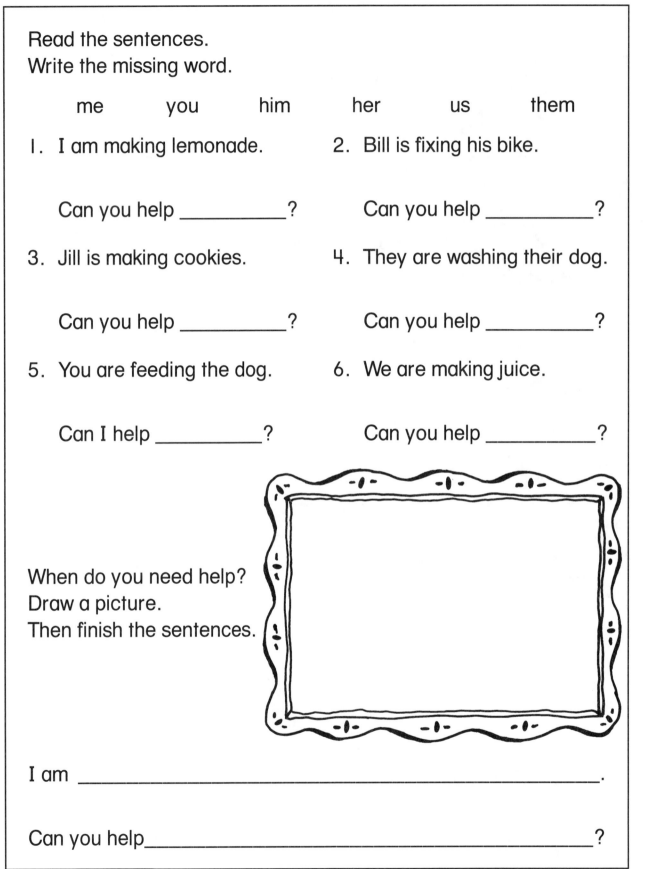

When do you need help?
Draw a picture.
Then finish the sentences.

I am _____.

Can you help_____?

(Supports Language Activities Big Book B, Activity 12) **Practicing key language: object pronouns**. Students complete questions using the pronouns listed at the top of the page. Then they draw themselves doing an activity they may need help with. They complete the sentences to go with their drawing.

Cut out these tangram pieces.

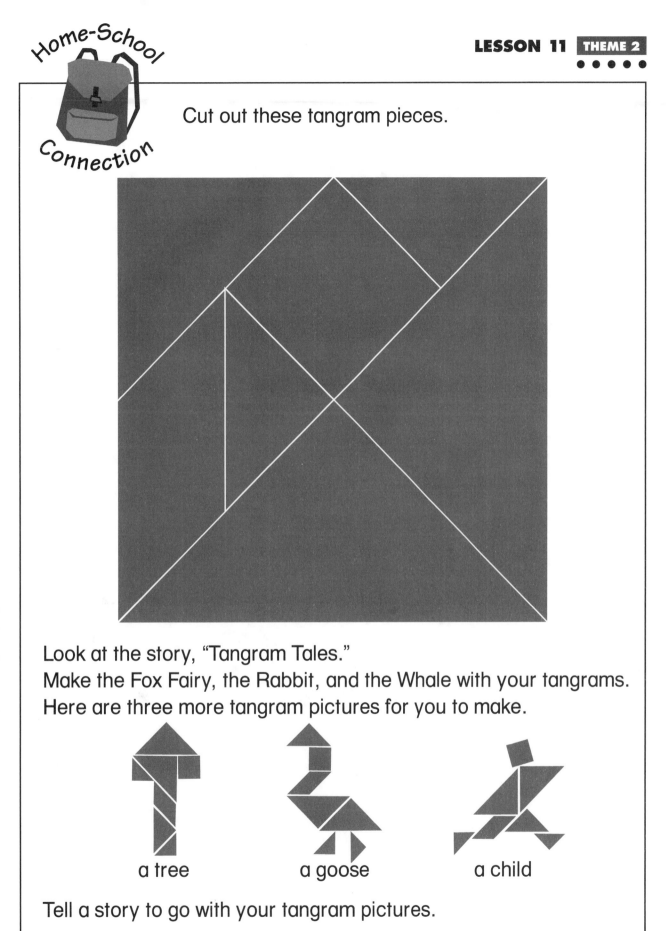

Look at the story, "Tangram Tales."

Make the Fox Fairy, the Rabbit, and the Whale with your tangrams.

Here are three more tangram pictures for you to make.

a tree   a goose   a child

Tell a story to go with your tangram pictures.

© Addison-Wesley Publishing Company

(Supports Student Book B, pages 21-23) **Home-School Connection; Constructing tangram pictures; telling an original story.** Students cut out the tangram pieces at the top of this page and use them to construct six tangram pictures. Tangram pictures of the Fox, the Rabbit and the Whale are found on pages 22-23 of the Student Book. Students can take home their tangram pieces and the tangram pictures on this page to share with their families.

Draw a beautiful forest.   Draw Anansi and his six sons.
Draw great flowers.   Draw the moon in the sky.
Draw wonderful trees.   Write about your picture.

(Supports Big Book: *How the Moon Got in the Sky*) **Following written directions; creative writing.** Students draw a scene following the written directions. Then they write about their picture on a separate piece of paper. You may want to save this page in the student's **Assessment Portfolio**.

Write each word under the correct picture.

tall	taller	tallest

_____   _____   _____

short	shorter	shortest

_____   _____   _____

(Supports Language Activities Big Book B, Activity 13) **Sequencing; practicing key language: comparative and superlative endings -er and -est.** Students write the correct word under each picture.

Some of the words in this story are missing. Read the words in the Word Box. Write the missing words on the lines.

One _____, Anansi the

_____ was in the

_____. He found something

_____ and beautiful.

It was a great circle of _____.

"How beautiful!" said _____.

"I will _____ it home. I will give it to one of

my six _____. But which one?" Anansi

couldn't _____.

WORD BOX		
Anansi	light	sons
decide	night	strange
forest	Spider	take

(Supports Big Book: *How the Moon Got in the Sky*) **Completing a cloze exercise using context clues; retelling a story.** Students complete the sentences, using the words provided in the Word Box. They then read the two paragraphs aloud to a partner and/or the teacher.

Home-School Connection

A. Write the story behind your name.

My first name is _____.

This is how I got my name. _____

_____

_____

_____

B. Make a hidden picture with your name. Have someone in your family find your name. Ask that person to draw a picture, too.

Can you find the name SUSAN in this picture?

Draw your name picture here.

32

(Supports Student Book B, page 28) **Home-School Connection.** After interviewing older members of their family, students write the story of how their name was chosen. Then students draw a name picture with the letters of their name hidden in the picture. An example is provided. Students take their story and their picture home to share with their families. They invite a family member to draw his or her own name picture. Ask students to bring this page back to class. You may want to save this page in the student's **Assessment Portfolio**.

sleeping	dolphin	bathroom	brother
eating	fox	bedroom	sister
tying my shoes	sandwich	kitchen	mother
grandparents	salad	living room	father

Reinforcing key vocabulary. Have students cut out the cards and match pictures with words. Students can use the set of cards (16 picture cards and 16 word cards) to play a game of Concentration alone or with a partner. As a variation, two students may combine their picture cards, or their word cards and lay out a Concentration game in which they will hunt for picture or word pairs. The picture and word cards on this page will also be used with the Amazing Words game board on page 35.

AMAZING WORDS

Put nine pictures on the game board.
Play an Amazing Words game.

Reinforcing key vocabulary. Each student chooses nine **picture cards** (provided on page 33) to glue on the game board. Two or three students play *Amazing Words* together. Players combine their sets of **word cards** from page 33 and place them face down on a table. In turn, each player picks up a word card and reads it aloud. If the matching picture appears on that player's game board, he or she places the word card on top of the picture. If not, the word card is returned to the table. The first player to fill his or her game board wins.

City Places

(Supports Language Activities Big Book B, Activity 14) **Reinforcing key vocabulary; following written directions.** Students play this game in small groups. Each group uses one game board and one die (or a set of number cards 1-6). Each player needs a game marker. Before beginning the game, each player writes the following Errand List on a piece of paper: TOY STORE, RESTAURANT, GAS STATION. The first player to visit and cross out all three places on the list and return HOME, wins the game.

What can you do? Put an X in the right box.

Yes, I can.   No, not yet.

1. Can you whistle? ☐ ☐

2. Can you spell your name backwards? ☐ ☐

3. Can you say "hello" in three languages? ☐ ☐

4. Can you count to ten in two languages? ☐ ☐

5. Can you say your phone number? ☐ ☐

6. Can you snap your fingers? ☐ ☐

7. Can you touch your toe to your ear? ☐ ☐

8. Can you count by tens to one hundred? ☐ ☐

Write two more things that you can do.

_____

_____

(Supports Student Book B, page 29) **Completing a questionnaire; providing information about self.**
Students answer the questionnaire by placing an X in the appropriate box: *Yes, I can.* or *No, not yet.* Then they
write two more things that they can do. Encourage students to write complete sentences. Allow ample time for
students to demonstrate some of the things they can do, and to teach the skill to other interested students.

Home-School Connection

	Sun.	Mon.	Tues.	Wed.	Thurs.	Fri.	Sat.

1. How many days are there in a week? _____

2. What's your favorite day? _____

3. How many days are there in this month? _____

4. How many Saturdays are in this month? _____

5. What do you do after school? What do you do on Saturdays? Write your plans on the calendar.

(Supports Language Activities Big Book B, Activity 15) **Home-School Connection; using a calendar.** Have students write the name of the present month at the top of this calendar and fill in the numbers for all the days. Be sure to start numbering on the correct day of the week! Have students answer the questions below the calendar. Provide help as needed. Encourage students to share responses to the last question before writing their plans on the calendar. Students may want to take this calendar home to share with their family.

Terrific Tarah!

We asked Tarah questions about herself and her life.
Here are four questions and four answers.
Draw a line from each question to the matching answer.

Question: What do you want to be when you grow up?

Tarah: It's fun. I like to race. I have lots of friends on my team.

Question: Who do you like best on Sesame Street?

Tarah: Yes! My favorite show was the one that was all about me. They showed a film of me in a wheelchair race.

Question: What do you like best about wheelchair sports?

Tarah: I want to be an actor while I'm a kid, then when I grow up I want to be a doctor.

Question: Do you have a favorite Sesame Street show?

Tarah: I like Big Bird best.

(Supports Reading Collection B, pages 30-32). **Matching questions and answers; drawing conclusions.**
Students read four interview questions addressed to Tarah, and her four answers. They draw lines connecting
each question with the appropriate answer. Then students work in pairs, interviewing each other. Help students prepare for their interviews by brainstorming a list of possible questions.

Write the words on the lines.

WORD BOX

ankle	ear	elbow	head
knee	shoulder	stomach	toe

(Supports Language Activities Big Book B, Activity 16) **Labeling a diagram; practicing key language.**
Students label parts of the body, using the words provided in the Word Box. Students can then work in pairs
and role play situations in which different parts of their body hurt. They can use the language presented in
Activity 16 and be quite dramatic! A: *I feel sick.* or *OW!* B: *What's the matter?* A: *My (ear) hurts.* etc. Encourage
each pair to present their favorite role play to the class.

We all lose our baby teeth. New teeth grow in their place. Ask your friends, "How many teeth have you lost?"

Name	How many lost teeth?
	🦷🦷🦷🦷🦷🦷🦷🦷
	🦷🦷🦷🦷🦷🦷🦷
	🦷🦷🦷🦷🦷🦷
	🦷🦷🦷🦷🦷🦷
	🦷🦷🦷🦷🦷🦷
	🦷🦷🦷🦷🦷🦷

(Supports Language Activities Big Book B, Activity 16) **Conducting a survey; graphing and analyzing data.**
Demonstrate how to enter information on the chart: students color in the number of lost teeth each classmate reports. For example, if Tom says he has lost 2 teeth, the student will write "Tom" on the line and color in the first two teeth in the row next to his name. Allow a set amount of time for students to conduct their survey, then analyze the results: *Who has lost the most teeth? How many teeth have most people lost?* etc.

Read each story. Check **Real** if it could really happen.
Check **Make-believe** if it could not really happen.

1. Ants walk outside. They look for food. They carry food to their ant hill.

Real ☐

Make-believe ☐

2. Little Ant ran home. Her mother was happy to see her. She made her tea and cookies.

Real ☐

Make-believe ☐

3. It is warm and sunny. The ants run out of their ant hill. They climb up trees and plants.

Real ☐

Make-believe ☐

4. A snowflake landed on Little Ant. A leaf landed on the snowflake. Little Ant said, "I want to go home."

Real ☐

Make-believe ☐

(Supports Big Book: *The Little Ant*) **Distinguishing between real and make-believe; drawing and supporting conclusions.** Students read each story and decide if it is Real or Make-Believe. You may want students to work with a partner. After students have completed the page, have them discuss and support their answers. Ask, *Why do you think it's real? Why do you think it's make-believe?*

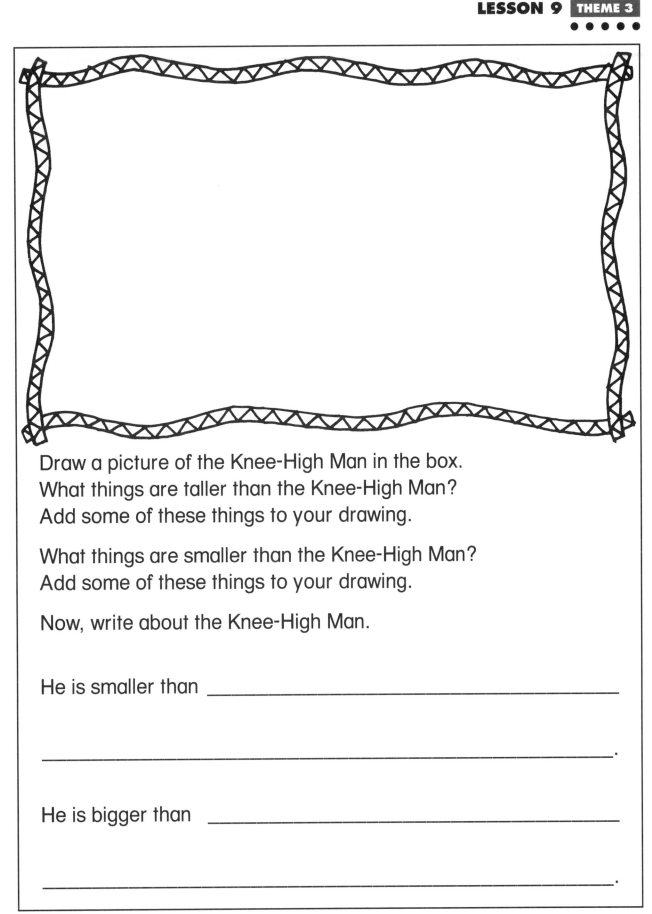

Draw a picture of the Knee-High Man in the box.
What things are taller than the Knee-High Man?
Add some of these things to your drawing.

What things are smaller than the Knee-High Man?
Add some of these things to your drawing.

Now, write about the Knee-High Man.

He is smaller than _____

_____.

He is bigger than _____

_____.

(Supports Student Book B, pages 34-38) **Extending story ideas; comparing.** Ask students to show you how tall a knee-high man is. (As high as their knee.) Write these two sentence starters on the board: *The Knee-High Man is smaller than.... The Knee-High Man is bigger than ....* Have students brainstorm a list of things to complete each sentence. Students then draw a scene of the Knee-High Man with some things that are bigger than he and some things that are smaller, and write sentences to go with their picture.

Work with a friend.
Write two things that are good about being small.

1. _____

_____

2. _____

_____

Write two things that are good about being big.

1. _____

_____

2. _____

_____

We did this page together.

_____   _____
    (*your name*)   (*your friend's name*)

(Supports Student Book B, pages 34-38) **Extending story ideas; creative problem solving; collaborative learning.** Students work with a partner and brainstorm three ways in which being small can be an advantage and three ways in which being big can be an advantage. Allow time for student partners to share their ideas with the rest of the class. You may want to save this page in the student's **Assessment Portfolio.**

Look at the pictures. Finish the sentences.

1. How many elephants were there in the morning?

   There $\frac{was}{were}$ <u>one</u>_____.

2. How many bears are there now?

   There $\frac{is}{are}$ _____.

3. How many dolls were there in the morning?

   There _____.

4. How many elephants are there now?

   There _____.

5. _____ two dolls now.

© Addison-Wesley Publishing Company

(Supports Language Activities Big Book B, Activity 17) **Comparing and contrasting; practicing key language.** Students examine the two pictures and answer the questions by circling the correct verb and writing the number word on the line. Discuss the answers and let students correct their work as needed. Have student pairs practice reading the completed questions and answers aloud to each other.

Find the matching picture.

_____ 1. He was taking care of the baby.

_____ 2. They were planting flowers.

_____ 3. They were painting.

_____ 4. They were cooking.

_____ 5. She was playing in the pool.

_____ 6. He was sweeping the porch.

(Supports Language Activities Big Book B, Activity 18) **Matching sentences and pictures; practicing key language.** Students read each sentence and find the matching picture. They write the letter of the picture on the line.

The Salt and Pepper Shake

and

and

Put your

On your

and

and

Put your

On your

and

and

Put your

On your

and

and

Put your

On your

Shake, shake, shake!
Shake all around.
Shake your body up and down!

(Supports Student Book B, page 39) **Home-School Connection.** Play "The Salt and Pepper Shake" and sing along. Have students track the words and pictures as they sing each verse. Have students practice singing the verses with a partner. Have half the class sing the verses while the other half does the actions, then reverse roles. Students can take this page home and teach "The Salt and Pepper Shake" to their families.

The Little Ant

Read each story. What will happen next?
Circle the best answer.

"It is spring" said Little Ant.
"May I play outside?"
Her mother answered, "It is still too cold for
a little ant to play outside."
Little Ant saw some snowflakes falling.

A. She went outside. Snow fell on her.

B. She played outside. She was warm.

Little Ant called for help. Finally
Little Ant's cousin, the flea heard her.

A. Little Ant played in the snow.

B. The flea came to help Little Ant.

(Supports Big Book: *The Little Ant*) **Drawing conclusions.** Students read each story and circle the sentence that tells what happens next. Have students share their answers and explain why that answer is best.

Listen to the story, *The Little Ant*.
Who does Little Ant talk to first?
Who does she talk to next?
Draw a line along the path.
Then, use the map to retell the story to a friend.

(Supports Big Book: *The Little Ant*) **Recalling sequence of story events; using a story map to retell a story.**
Students reread or listen to the story of *The Little Ant* and then recall the story events as you ask: *Who does Little Ant talk to first? Who does she talk to next?* As they answer each question, they draw a line along the path of the story map. Then, they use their story map to retell the story to a partner, the teacher, and/or their families.

Imagine that Little Ant and Little Bee pushed and pushed the stone, but it was too heavy to move. What could they do next?

Work with a partner.
Write two new endings for the story.
Then put a star by the ending you like best.

1. _____

_____

_____

_____

2. _____

_____

_____

_____

We did this page together.

_____   _____
(*your name*)   (*your friend's name*)

(Supports Student Book B, pages 40-41) **Creative problem solving; drawing conclusions, collaborative learning.** Students work in pairs. Together they think up two different resolutions to the story and write the new story endings on the lines. Allow time for students to share their favorite original ending with the class. You may want to save this page in the student's **Assessment Portfolio**.

Make a Pinwheel

Make this pinwheel with your family.
You will need scissors, a pencil with an eraser, and a straight pin.
Follow the directions.

Blow on your pinwheel. Can you make it spin?
How else can you make it spin?

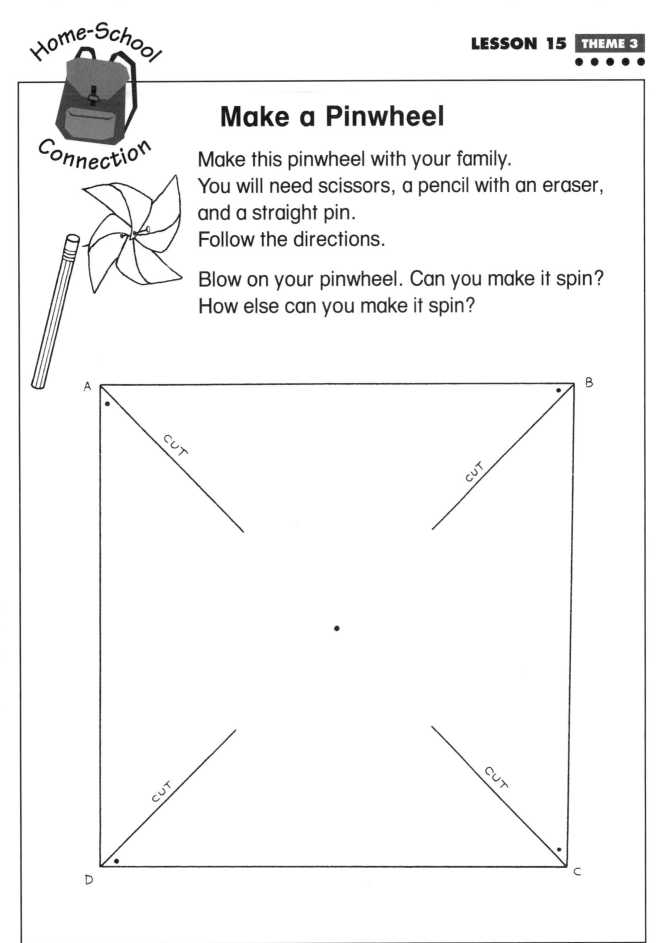

(Supports Student Book B, page 42) **Home-School Connection.** Ask students to blow on their finger. Then ask, *Can you feel the air? Where does the air come from? (Your lungs.)* Then read and discuss the directions. Students can make the pinwheel in class or take the page home and make it with their families. To make the pinwheel, each student will need a straight pin and a pencil with an eraser. After pinwheels are made, ask: *How can you make the pinwheel spin?* Encourage students to think of lots of different answers.

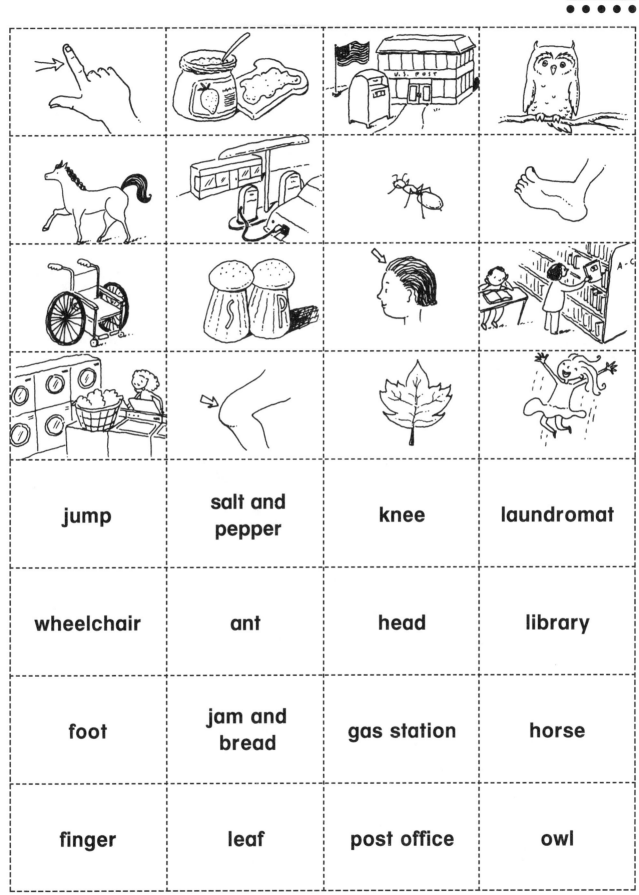

jump	salt and pepper	knee	laundromat
wheelchair	ant	head	library
foot	jam and bread	gas station	horse
finger	leaf	post office	owl

Reinforcing key vocabulary. Have students cut out the cards and match pictures with words. Students can use the set of cards (16 picture cards and 16 word cards) to play a game of Concentration alone or with a partner. As a variation, two students may combine their picture cards, or their word cards and lay out a Concentration game in which they will hunt for picture or word pairs. The picture and word cards on this page will also be used with the Amazing Words game board on page 55.

AMAZING WORDS

Put nine pictures on the game board.
Play an Amazing Words game.

Reinforcing key vocabulary. Each student chooses nine **picture cards** (provided on page 53) to glue on the game board. Two or three students play *Amazing Words* together. Players combine their sets of **word cards** from page 53 and place them face down on a table. In turn, each player picks up a word card and reads it aloud. If the matching picture appears on that player's game board, he or she places the word card on top of the picture. If not, the word card is returned to the table. The first player to fill his or her game board wins.

Help these busy bees make a hive of compound words.

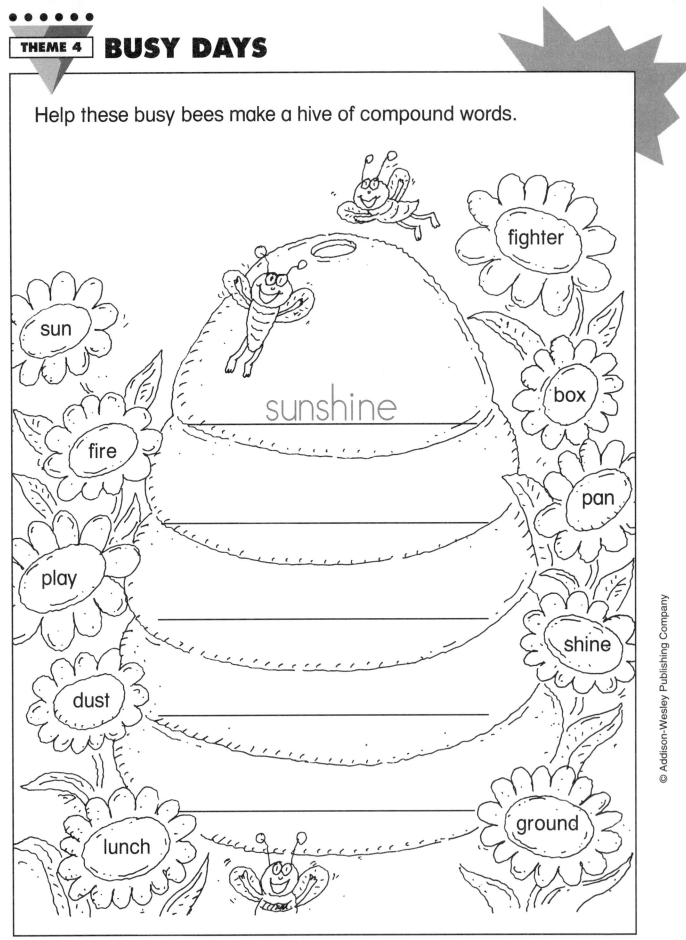

(Supports Student Book B, page 43) **Word study in context: compound words.** Write the words *homework* and *dustpan* on the board. Say, *These are compound words, each word is made of two smaller words pushed together.* Have volunteers identify the two words in each compound word. Have students work in pairs to complete this page. Students construct compound words by combining a word on the left side of the page with one on the right side. They write the compound word on a line in the beehive.

Crossword Puzzle

Across
1. A mail carrier _____ the mail.
6. A trash collector _____ trash.
7. A _____ reports the news.
8. A _____ serves people their food.

Down
2. A _____ types letters.
3. A clerk _____ in a store.
4. A _____ works in a hospital.
5. A baseball _____ plays baseball.

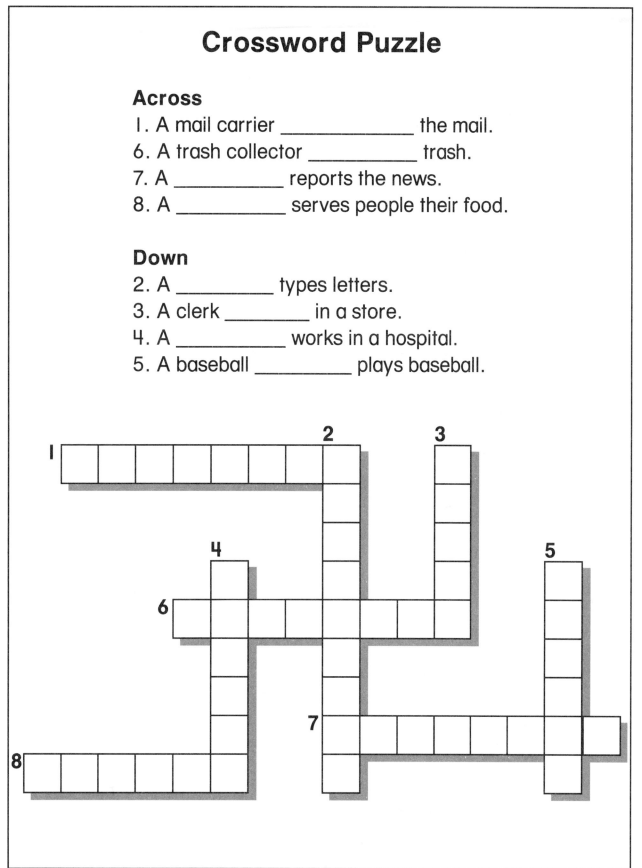

(Supports Language Activities Big Book B, Activity 20) **Completing sentences; practicing key vocabulary.**
Students read the first item ACROSS. One student gives the answer: delivers. Students write the word
delivers, one letter to a box in the puzzle. They continue with other items in the same way.

Write the sentences.

1. sell She doesn't sell shoes.

She sells apples.

2. cut She _____

_____

3. drive They _____

_____

4. play He _____

_____

5. deliver They _____

_____

(Supports Language Activities Big Book B, Activity 21) **Writing complete sentences; practicing key vocabulary.** Students write two complete sentences in the simple present, negative and affirmative, based on the illustrations for each item.

Occupations Alphabet

Work with a friend. Write the name of a job that begins with each letter of the alphabet. Good luck!

a _____   n _____

b _____   o _____

c _____   p _____

d _____   q _____

e _____   r _____

f _____   s _____

g _____   t _____

h _____   u _____

i _____   v _____

j _____   w _____

k _____   x _____

l _____   y _____

m _____   z _____

How many job names did you write? _____
Circle the occupation you like best.

We did this page together.

_____   _____
         (*your name*)   (*your friend's name*)

(Supports Student Book B, pages 44-46) **Classifying, alphabetizing, working collaboratively.** Students work in pairs or in small groups. They try to think of an occupation title beginning with each letter of the alphabet. Allow ample time for classmates to share, compare, and add to their lists. Have students count the number of job titles on their list and circle the occupation that they like best.

59

Find the matching picture.

a b c d

e f g h

___g___ 1. It chases the bird.

_____ 2. The baby kisses the dog.

_____ 3. The boy watches the football game.

_____ 4. It chases the mail carrier.

_____ 5. He catches the football.

_____ 6. She kisses the baby.

_____ 7. It catches the stick.

_____ 8. The dog watches TV.

(Supports Language Activities Big Book B, Activity 22) **Matching sentences and pictures.** Students read the sentences and find the matching pictures. They write the letter of the picture on the line at the beginning of the sentence.

Answer the questions.

I. When does she get up?

She gets up at 7:00.

2. What does she wash?

_____

3. What does she make for lunch?

_____

4. Who does she kiss?

_____

5. What does she catch?

_____

6. When does she get to school?

_____

7. Where does she play before school?

_____

(Supports Language Activities Big Book B, Activity 23) **Writing complete sentences; practicing key language.** Students write complete sentences to answer the questions, using the pictures on the right as cues. Discuss fully after completion; check for s/es endings on the verbs. You may want to save this page in the student's **Assessment Portfolio**.

Home-School Connection

What do you do every day? Write three things.

1. Every day I _____

2. Every day I _____

3. Every day I _____

Talk to someone in your family. Write three things she or he does every day.

1. _____

_____

2. _____

_____

3. _____

Write two things you do together almost every week.

_____

_____

(Supports Student Book B, page 47) **Home-School Connection.** Students discuss things they do everyday, then each student completes the top section of this page. Each student takes the page home, interviews one member of the family and lists three things he or she does every day. The family member helps the student think of two things they do together almost every week. Ask students to bring the page back to school. You may want to save this page in the student's **Assessment Portfolio**.

Yummy, Yummy

I love, I love potatoes,
I love them every way.
Roasty, toasty, mashed or smashed,
Potatoes really make my day!

Yummy, yummy in my tummy,
Yummy, yummy, yum!
I love potatoes every way,
Potatoes really make my day!

Write your own verse.

I love, I love _____

I love _____ every way.

_____

_____

_____ really make my day!

(Supports Big Book: *Only a Nickel*) **Creating original song verses.** Brainstorm ideas for new verses. Use some of these foods in the first line: *ice cream, sandwiches, fresh fruit, vegetables, cookies.* The third line of the verse can list specific flavors or types: *vanilla, cookie dough, double fudge; in a cup or in a cone.* Have students note if the food word in the first line ends in s. This determines whether the pronoun **it** or **they** is used in the second line. Students may choose to write a new verse or copy a class verse.

Find the matching picture.

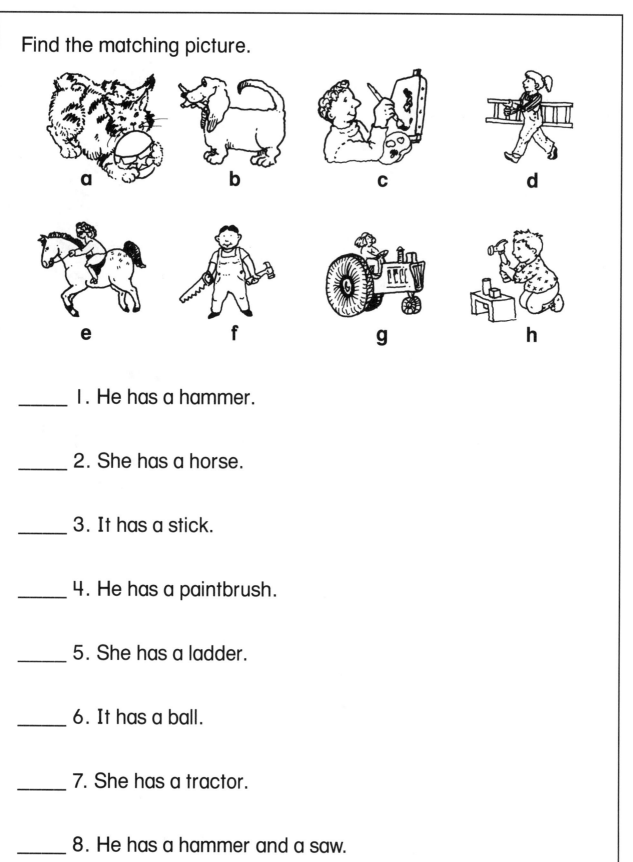

_____ 1. He has a hammer.

_____ 2. She has a horse.

_____ 3. It has a stick.

_____ 4. He has a paintbrush.

_____ 5. She has a ladder.

_____ 6. It has a ball.

_____ 7. She has a tractor.

_____ 8. He has a hammer and a saw.

(Supports Language Activities Big Book B, Activity 24) **Matching sentences and pictures.** Students read the sentences and find the matching pictures. They write the letter of the picture on the line at the beginning of the sentence.

Read the story. Then read the questions.
Choose the best answer.

Dr. Jackson is a very busy person.
Every morning he goes to a hospital and
visits sick people. He helps them a lot. He
stays there three hours from 9:00 to
12:00. Then he eats lunch. After lunch,
he goes to his office to see more sick
people. He stays there until 5:00. Then
he goes home, tired but happy.

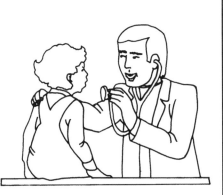

1. Where does Dr. Jackson
   work?

   ◯ In a hospital.

   ◯ In a bank.

   ◯ In a house.

2. How many hours does he
   stay in the hospital?

   ◯ One hour.

   ◯ Thirty minutes.

   ◯ Three hours.

3. What time does he go home?

   ◯ Three o'clock.

   ◯ Four o'clock.

   ◯ Five o'clock.

4. Does he like his work?

   ◯ Yes, he does.

   ◯ No, he doesn't.

   ◯ He never goes to work.

(Supports Language Activities Big Book B, Activity 25) **Identifying details; making inferences.** Students
read the story and answer each question, filling in the ovals next to their choices. You may want to save this
page in the student's **Assessment Portfolio.**

Ask your friends, "What do you want to be when you grow up?" Write the name of the job. Have your friend write his or her initials next to the job.

Jobs

What do <u>you</u> want to be when you grow up?

_____

What do you need to learn in order to do that job?

_____

_____

(Supports Language Activities Big Book B, Activity 25) **Taking a survey; recording and analyzing data.** Review the directions with the students. Allow a set period of time for students to conduct their survey. When the surveys are completed, encourage students to discuss and compare results. What was the most popular job on each student's survey? How many different jobs were listed all together? Have students complete the questions at the bottom of the page and share their responses with the class.

My Visit With Johnny Appleseed

Johnny Appleseed met many people and animals while planting apple seeds. Pretend that you are a pioneer or a forest animal. Write about your visit with Johnny. Draw a picture to go with your story.

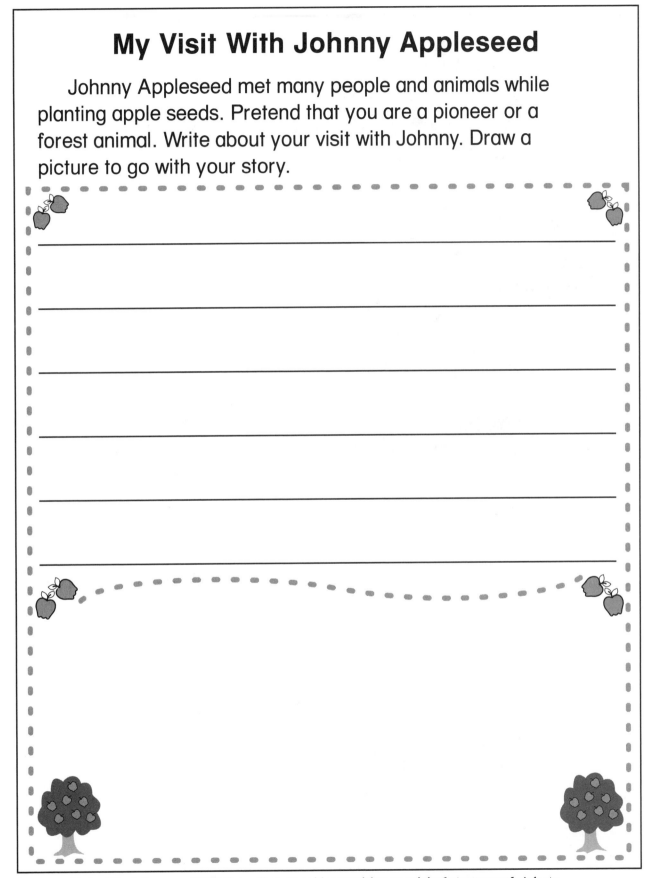

(Supports Student Book B, pages 48-51) **Extending story ideas; writing an original story sequel.** Ask students to recall and infer information about Johnny Appleseed. *What did he do? What was he like? How did he travel? What did he carry with him?* Write the students' responses on the board. These ideas may be helpful to students as they write about their imaginary visit with Johnny Appleseed. You may want to save this page in the student's **Assessment Portfolio**.

Look at the picture.
Write the math story.

1.

There were _____ doughnuts.

Pig took _____ doughnut.

Now there are _____ doughnuts left.

2.

There were _____ potatoes.

Bear took _____ potato.

Now there are _____ potatoes left.

3.

There was _____ nickel.

Bear took _____ nickel.

Now there are _____ nickels left.

(Supports Big Book: *Only a Nickel*) **Extending story ideas; writing and solving math stories.** Students use the picture cues to complete and solve subtraction math stories. They read the math stories aloud to a partner. Students can write other similar math stories about picture scenes in the Big Book, *Only a Nickel.*

You have 70¢ to spend at the fair.
What will you buy?
Write a list.
Be sure you can pay for everything!

My Shopping List

price

_____ ____¢

_____ ____¢

_____ ____¢

_____ ____¢

_____ ____¢

Total ____

(Supports Big Book: *Only a Nickel*) **Reviewing key vocabulary: money; solving an open-ended math problem.** Review the directions with the students. Have students name each item in the scene and identify the price. Then have students complete their shopping list as they wish. Remind them that they have only 70 cents to spend. Circulate around the room, providing help as needed. Encourage students to show their shopping lists to classmates and compare the choices.

What can your magnet pull?
Check **YES** or **NO**.

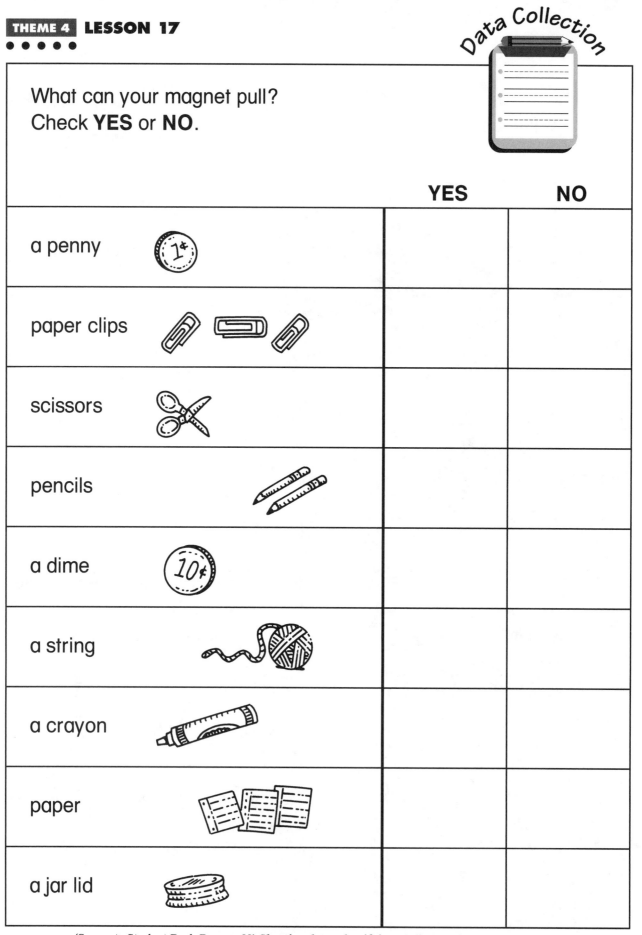

		YES	NO
a penny			
paper clips			
scissors			
pencils			
a dime			
a string			
a crayon			
paper			
a jar lid			

(Supports Student Book B, page 62) **Charting data; classifying.** Collect several magnets and the materials that appear on this chart. Small groups of students can take turns experimenting with the magnets and materials. Students test each object to see if the magnet pulls it or not. They put a check in the YES or NO column. Students may want to gather additional materials to test with a magnet. They can make their own similar chart.

astronaut	nickel	doctor	reporter
dentist	dime	hospital	waiter
factory worker	paper clips	firefighter	clerk
penny	scissors	police officer	carpenter

Reinforcing key vocabulary. Have students cut out the cards and match pictures with words. Students can use the set of cards (16 picture cards and 16 word cards) to play a game of Concentration alone or with a partner. As a variation, two students may combine their picture cards, or their word cards and lay out a Concentration game in which they will hunt for picture or word pairs. The picture and word cards on this page will also be used with the Amazing Words game board on page 73.

AMAZING WORDS

Put nine pictures on the game board.
Play an Amazing Words game.

Reinforcing key vocabulary. Each student chooses nine **picture cards** (provided on page 71) to glue on the game board. Two or three students play *Amazing Words* together. Players combine their sets of **word cards** from page 71 and place them face down on a table. In turn, each player picks up a word card and reads it aloud. If the matching picture appears on that player's game board, he or she places the word card on top of the picture. If not, the word card is returned to the table. The first player to fill his or her game board wins.

73

AROUND THE POND

In the woods	On a farm	In a pond

rabbit	bird	bear	deer
horse	cow	turtle	goat
hen	frog	beaver	fish

74

(Supports Language Activities Big Book B, Activity 27) **Classifying.** Students decide where each of the animals live and then write the name of the animal in the appropriate column. They can add the names of other animals they know as well.

Think about summer.
What can you see and hear and smell in summer?
What do animals do in the summer? What do people do?
Make a list poem about summer.
Draw pictures to go with your poem.

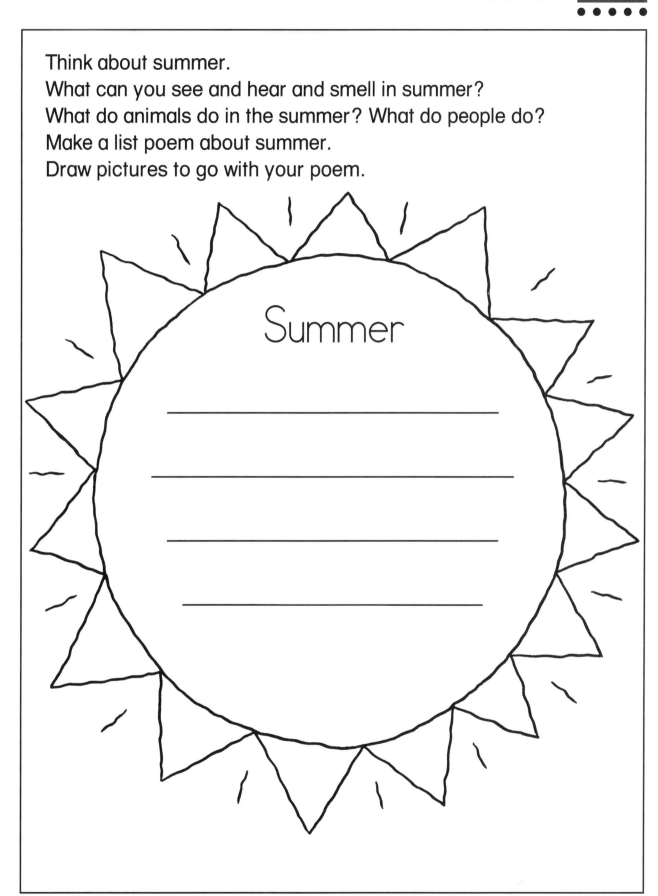

Summer

_____

_____

_____

_____

(Supports Student Book B, page 55) **Writing an original poem.** Have students brainstorm a list of summer sights, sounds, smells and activities. Write their ideas on a chart. Each child then writes and illustrates his or her own list poem about summer. You may want to save this page in the student's **Assessmet Portfolio**.

Write a "Tell Me Why" story.

Circle one thing from each box.

Then write the words on the lines on page 77. Follow the code!

Read your "Tell Me Why" story to a friend.

♥
| cat | elephant |
| snake | swan | giraffe |

✚
| tails | noses | necks | bodies |

❀
| mountains | pond | forest |

✱
| Tricky Fox | Magic Mosquito |
| Clever Monkey | Powerful Parrot |

★
| pulled and pulled | grabbed and stretched |
| tickled and twisted |

(Supports Student Book B, pages 56-60) **Following directions, developing an understanding of *pourquoi* story structure; understanding cause and effect.** Students choose one item from each box and write that word or phrase on the lines on page 77 marked with the appropriate symbol. They then illustrate the resulting story with a "before" and "after" picture of the starring animal. Students read their "Tell Me Why" to a friend and/or the teacher.

Long ago ♥ _____ S had

short ✚ _____. They lived in

the ✿ _____.

One day a ♥ _____ met

a ✳ _____ in the

✿ _____. The ✳ _____

★ _____

the ♥ _____ 'S ✚ _____.

Now all ♥ _____ S have

long ✚ _____ .

Draw a picture of your animal.

Before	After

Follow these directions.

1. The farmer is going to milk the cow.
   Draw the cow in the barn.

2. The farmer's son is going to drive
   the truck. Draw the son in the truck.
   Color the truck green.

3. The farmer's daughter is going to feed
   the pigs. Draw three more pigs in the pen.
   Color them pink.

(Supports Language Activities Big Book B, Activity 28-29) **Following written directions.** Students need crayons to complete this page. They color and add to the scene as they read and follow written directions. Then they practice with a partner, asking and answering information questions, *Who's this? Where's the farmer? What's he going to do?*

Now plan a trip with your class. Discuss where
you could go. List a few possibilities.

_____   _____   _____

_____   _____   _____

_____   _____   _____

Now take a vote. Decide where you want to go.
Then write about your trip.

We're going to _____.

We're going on _____.
                              (day)

We're going by _____.
                    (transportation)

We'll get to _____ at _____.

We're going to _____.

Then we'll _____.

It's going to be a _____ day!

(Supports Language Activities Big Book B, Activity 28-29) **Working collaboratively; writing a report.**
Students work together to plan a real or imaginary field trip. Each student writes a report about the up-com-
ing or imaginary trip.

frog   **turtle**   **fish**

Work with a friend. Write down your ideas.

1. How are turtles and frogs alike? _____

_____

2. How are turtles and frogs different? _____

_____

3. How are turtles and fish alike? _____

_____

4. How are turtles and fish different? _____

_____

We did this page together.

_____   _____
        (*your name*)   (*your friend's name*)

(Supports Student Book B, page 61) **Comparing and contrasting.** Students work with a partner. They list at least one way in which turtles and frogs are alike and at least one way in which they are different. They then compare and contrast turtles and fish. Allow plenty of time for students to share their responses with their classmates and appreciate the wide variety of ideas.

Ask your friends, "What is your favorite pet?"
Write the name of the animal. Write your friend's initials
in the box next to the animal's name. When your survey
is done, color in all the boxes with initials.

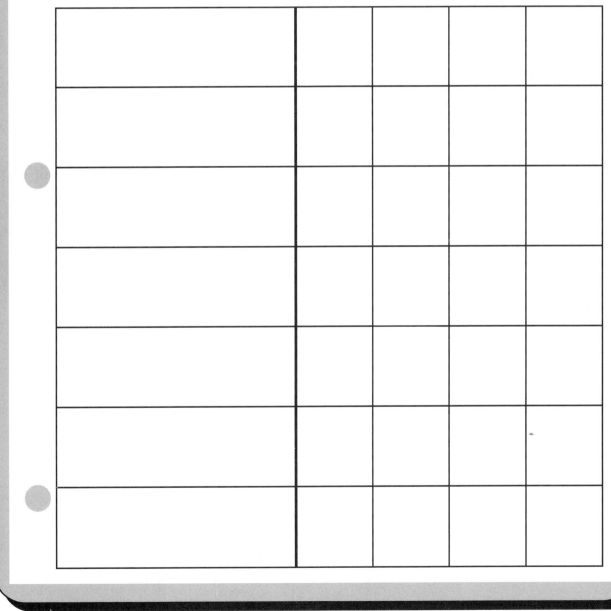

Favorite Pets   **Write initials here.**

(Supports Language Activities Big Book B, Activity 30) **Taking a survey; graphing and analyzing data.**
Review the directions and the names of the animals shown on the page. Allow a set amount of time for students to conduct their survey. Then have students color in the boxes with initials to create a bar graph. Ask, *Which pet was the most popular in your survey?* Encourage classmates to compare and discuss their survey results.

Design Your Own Beaver Lodge.

You need a door, a place for food, and a place to sleep.
What will you use to build your lodge?

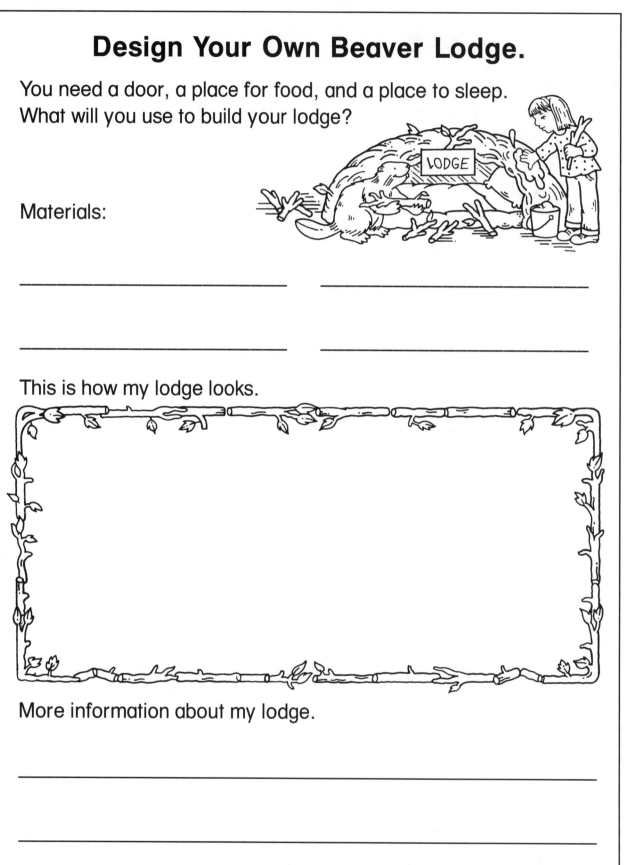

Materials:

_____   _____

_____   _____

This is how my lodge looks.

More information about my lodge.

_____

_____

(Supports Student Book B, pages 62-64) **Drawing and labeling a diagram; creative problem solving.** Have students discuss the diagram of the beaver lodge on Student Book page 63. Ask, *What materials do beavers use to build a lodge? Where do beavers keep their food? Where do they eat and sleep? Where is the door to the lodge?* Tell students they will draw and label their own diagram of a beaver lodge. They can use any materials they wish, not just branches and mud. Have students brainstorm ideas before they write and draw.

What do beavers have to do every day?
Write four complete sentences.

1. <u>Beavers have to</u> _____

   _____

2. _____

   _____

3. _____

   _____

4. _____

   _____

(Supports Language Activities Big Book B, Activity 31) **Practicing key language; applying story and picture information.** Students use picture cues and background knowledge to write four statements about beavers. Remind students that a sentence begins with a capital letter and ends with a period. Allow time for students to read their statements aloud to each other.

Home-School Connection

El Coquí
A lullaby from Puerto Rico

El Coquí sings a sweet song at twilight.
He is singing as sleep comes to me.
When I wake all alone in the moonlight,
El Coquí sings good night from the tree.

Coquí, Coquí, Coquí, quí, quí, quí,
Coquí, Coquí, Coquí, quí, quí, quí.

© Addison-Wesley Publishing Company

(Supports Student Book B, page 65) **Home-School Connection; following oral directions.** Have students
add to and color the picture according to your directions: *Draw a red bird on a branch next to a coquí. Draw a
purple flower under the tree. Draw an orange butterfly above the flower. Color four coquíes dark green. Color
two coquíes light green.* Have students practice reading and singing the words to the song. Students can take
this page home and share the song with their families.

The coquíes are having a race. Help them get to the finish line. Work with a friend. Write a word in each box that begins with the letter in the box. The word should be something about a coquí.

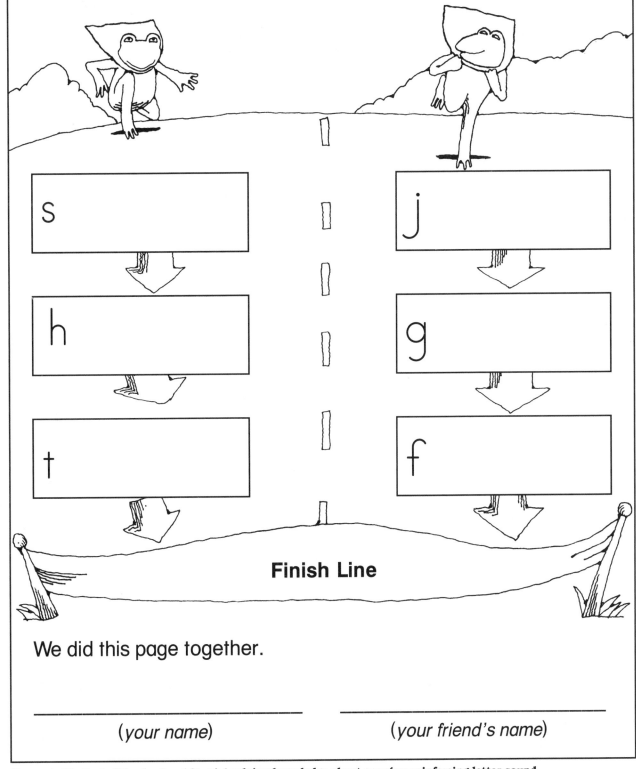

s

h

t

j

g

f

Finish Line

We did this page together.

_____   _____
(*your name*)   (*your friend's name*)

(Supports Big Book: *Why the Coquí Sings*) **Applying knowledge about coquíes; reinforcing letter-sound associations.** Students must write words beginning with *s*, *h*, and *t* in order to get Coquí #1 to the finish line. They must write words beginning with *j*, *g*, and *f* in order to get Coquí #2 to the finish line. With the class, brainstorm words that describe what coquíes look like, what they do, how they move, where they live. Students can continue to brainstorm in pairs, as they choose words to write beginning with the letters *s*, *h*, *t*, *j*, *g*, and *f*.

What do they have to do every day?

1. _____

2. _____

3. _____

4. _____

5. _____

What do <u>you</u> have to do every day?

I have to _____

(Supports Language Activities Big Book B, Activity 32) **Writing descriptive sentences; practicing key language: *have to, has to.*** Students refer to five pictures as they answer the question, *What do they have to do every day?* They then draw a picture showing something they themselves have to do every day and write a sentence describing it. You may want to save this page in the student's **Assessment Portfolio**.

Home-School Connection

PEPITO

(Supports Big Book: *Why the Coqui Sings*) **Home-School Connection; making a take-home book.** Students color, cut out, and paste pictures on separate sheets of paper. They put the pictures in the proper sequence. Then they write story text to go with each picture. Students may retell the story in their own words, or they may copy text from the Big Book. Students create book covers and staple their books together. They practice reading their book to a partner and/or teacher before taking it home to share with their family.

Write the right word on the line.

The King called a meeting

In the _____ of the trees.
(shade, shed)

The animals _____ running
(same, came)

Even tiny coquíes.

"To pep you all up

I'm holding a _____
(race, rice)

Tomorrow at sunset

In this very _____."
(plate, place)

The little coquíes

All thought of a _____.
(plane, plan)

"We can win the big race

We're sure that we _____."
(can, cane)

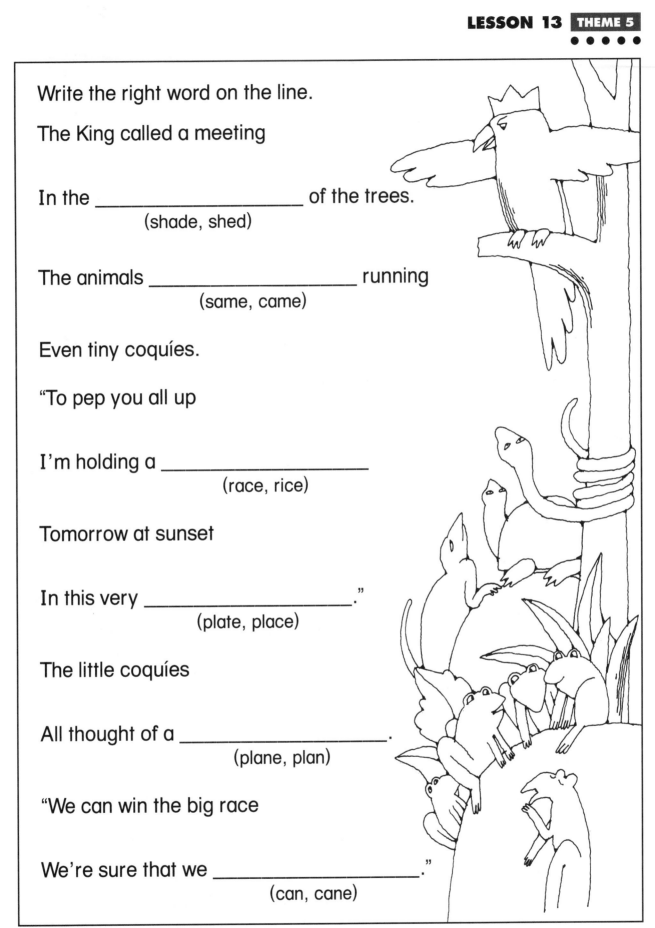

(Supports Big Book:, *Why the Coquí Sings*) **Completing a cloze exercise; word analysis in context: silent** *e.*
Remind students of the "silent *e* rule" by writing word pairs such as man/mane, pin/pine, hop/hope on the
board for students to read and discuss. Have students complete this page independently or working in pairs.
Correct the page together, and encourage students to read the verses aloud to each other.

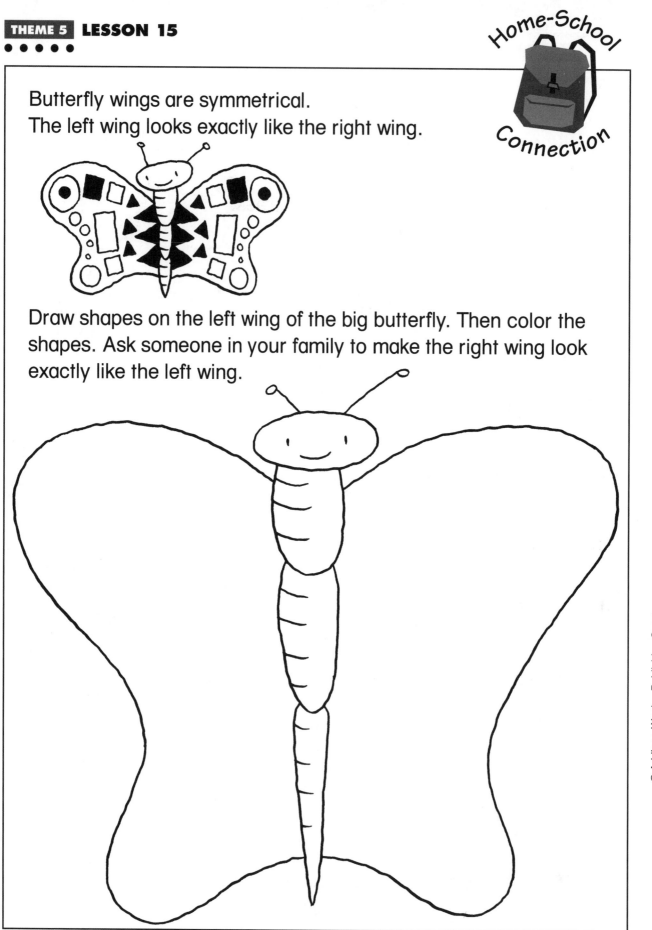

Butterfly wings are symmetrical.
The left wing looks exactly like the right wing.

Draw shapes on the left wing of the big butterfly. Then color the shapes. Ask someone in your family to make the right wing look exactly like the left wing.

(Supports Student Book B, page 68) **Home-School Connection; reviewing shapes; exploring symmetry.**
Draw attention to the little butterfly. *What shapes do you see on the butterfly's wings? How many (circles) do you see on the left wing? On the right wing?* Have students draw and color in their own shapes and patterns on the left wing of the big butterfly. They take this page home and invite a family member to color the right wing of the big butterfly to match.

Home-School Connection

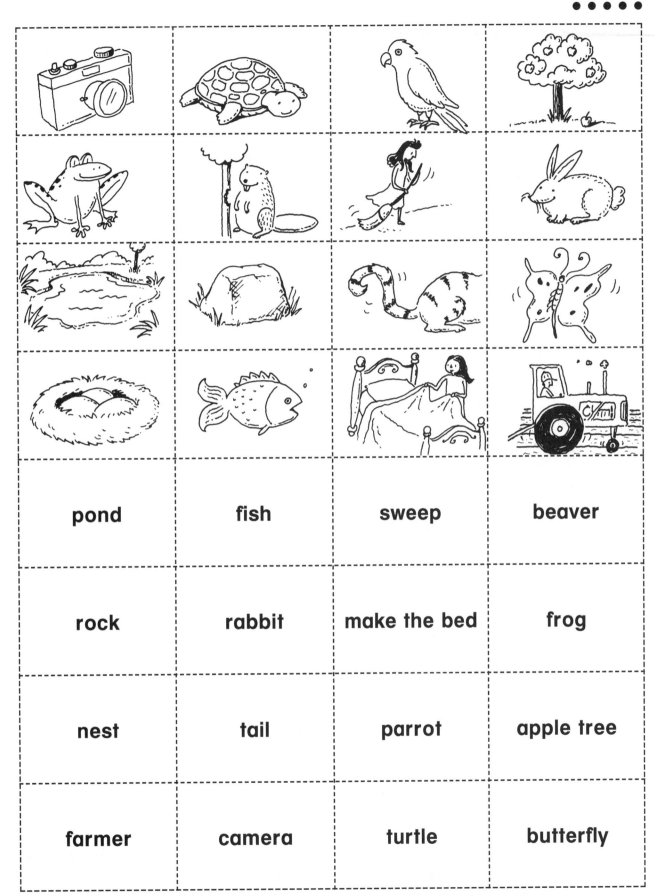

pond	fish	sweep	beaver
rock	rabbit	make the bed	frog
nest	tail	parrot	apple tree
farmer	camera	turtle	butterfly

Reinforcing key vocabulary. Have students cut out the cards and match pictures with words. Students can use the set of cards (16 picture cards and 16 word cards) to play a game of Concentration alone or with a partner. As a variation, two students may combine their picture cards, or their word cards and lay out a Concentration game in which they will hunt for picture or word pairs. The picture and word cards on this page will also be used with the Amazing Words game board on page 93.

91

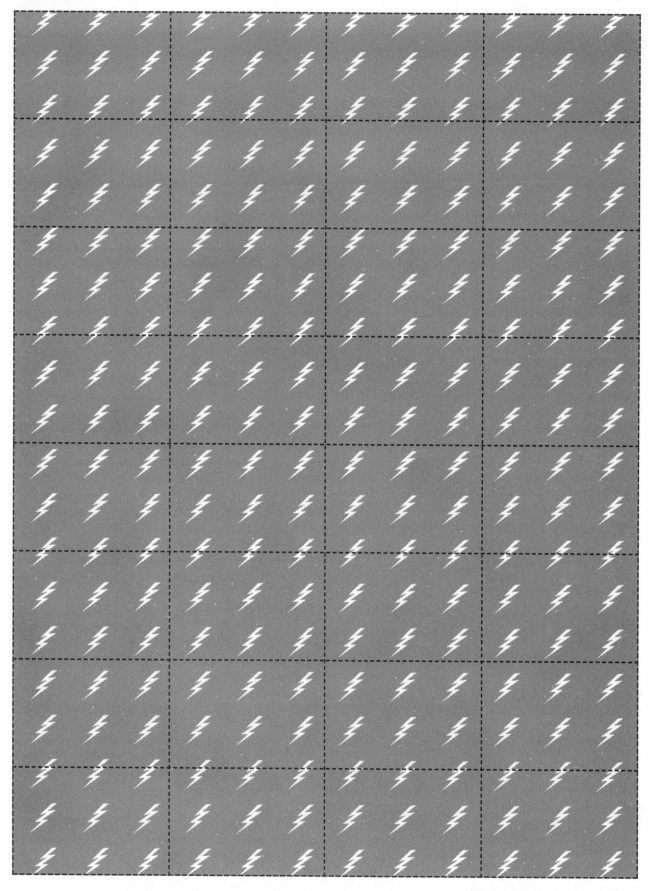

AMAZING WORDS

Put nine pictures on the game board.
Play an Amazing Words game.

Reinforcing key vocabulary. Each student chooses nine **picture cards** (provided on page 91) to glue on the game board. Two or three students play *Amazing Words* together. Players combine their sets of **word cards** from page 91 and place them face down on a table. In turn, each player picks up a word card and reads it aloud. If the matching picture appears on that player's game board, he or she places the word card on top of the picture. If not, the word card is returned to the table. The first player to fill his or her game board wins.

NATURE WALK

(Supports Language Activities Big Book B, Activity 33) **Sequencing.** Students discuss each picture, and then number the pictures to show the sequence of events in the life cycle and journey of an apple: from seed to tree to harvest to store, where it is bought and eaten by a customer. Encourage students to describe the chain of events using the numbered pictures as cues.

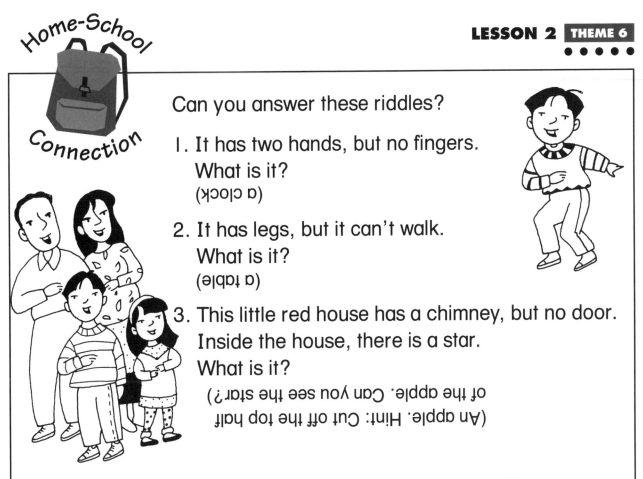

Can you answer these riddles?

1. It has two hands, but no fingers.
   What is it?
   (a clock)

2. It has legs, but it can't walk.
   What is it?
   (a table)

3. This little red house has a chimney, but no door.
   Inside the house, there is a star.
   What is it?
   (An apple. Hint: Cut off the top half of the apple. Can you see the star?)

Ask your family to help you think of a riddle or a joke. Write it here. Share it with your class.

_____

_____

_____

_____

_____

_____

(Supports Student Book B, page 69) **Home-School Connection; understanding and telling riddles and jokes.** Read and discuss the riddles together. If possible, bring an apple to class so you can demonstrate the "star in the apple" riddle. Encourage students to share other riddles they know. Students take this page home and with family help, write down a riddle or joke. Ask students to bring the page back to school so they can share their new riddle or joke with the class.

Classes Under the Trees

Draw your class under the trees.

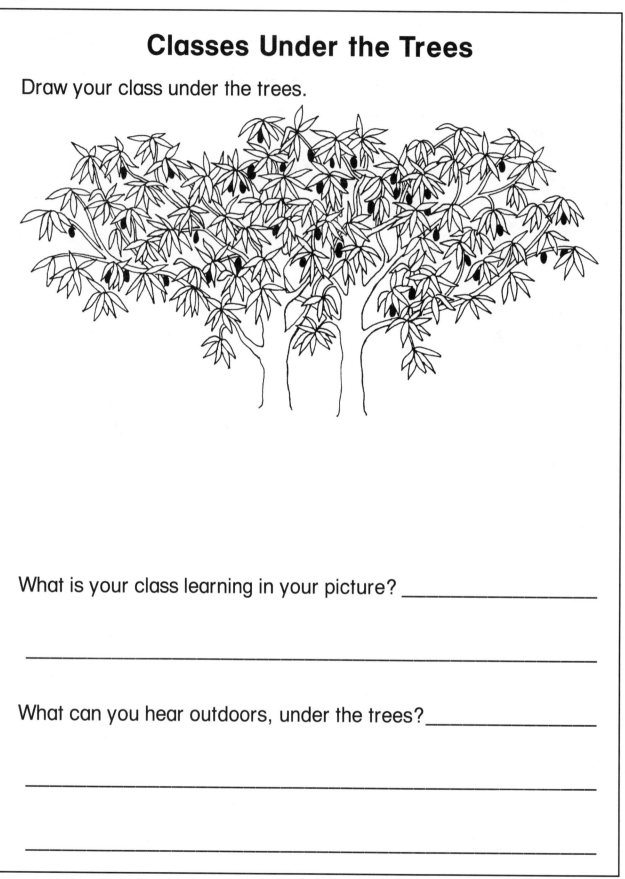

What is your class learning in your picture? _____

_____

What can you hear outdoors, under the trees?_____

_____

_____

(Supports Student Book B, pages 70-71) **Extending and personalizing story concepts.** Ask students, *Would you like to have classes outside, under the trees. What would you like to learn about outside?* Have student draw their own class under the trees, then answer the questions below. You may want to save this page in the student's **Assessment Portfolio**.

Write the sentences.

1. laugh

She didn't laugh at the clown.

She laughed at the monkey.

2. park

He

3. fix

They

4. miss

He

(Supports Language Activities Big Book B, Activity 34) **Practicing simple past tense, positive and negative statements; writing complete sentences.** Students use picture cues to write sentences. They write a negative past tense sentence about the picture on the left and a positive sentence about the picture on the right. As sentences are read aloud after completion, stress the -t end sound of these past tense verbs.

Look at the picture.
Write the missing word in the sentence.

1. walk   2. pick   3. chase

4. fix   5. brush   6. cook

This is what a farm family did last Saturday.

1. In the morning, Grandpa _____walked_____ in the woods.

2. Judy and Tom _____ strawberries.

3. The baby _____ the chickens out in the yard.

4. Mom and Dad _____ the fence near the barn.

5. Jean and Patrick _____ the horses.

6. At 6:00 Grandma and Grandpa _____ chicken on the grill.

(Supports Language Activities Big Book B, Activity 35) **Constructing simple past tense; completing sentences.** Students complete the story by looking at the illustration that goes with each sentence and writing the past tense of the given verb on the line provided. Encourage students to read the completed story to a partner and ask and answer questions about the pictures.

1. Write these words on the map.

   North America   Africa
   South America   Asia
   Australia   Antarctica
   Europe   Equator

2. Where do you live? Draw a star ★ on the map.

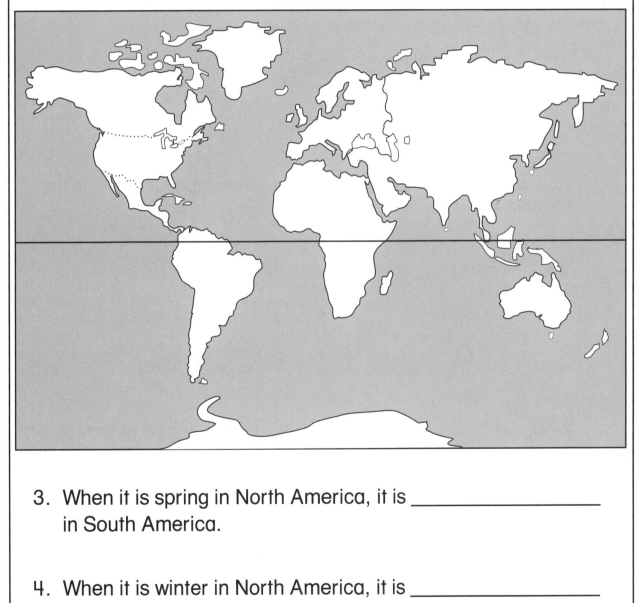

3. When it is spring in North America, it is _____ in South America.

4. When it is winter in North America, it is _____ in Australia.

(Supports Big Book: *Here It's Winter*) **Labeling a map; applying information from the story.** Display a world map and help students locate and read the names of the seven continents, and the equator. Have a volunteer locate where you live on the classroom world map. Students can work with a partner as they label the map on this page with the names of the continents. They will also label the equator, draw a star on the place where they live, and answer the questions at the bottom of the page. Provide help as needed.

Read the story. Then read the questions. Choose the best answer.

My name is Tina.

My Mom and Dad had a two-week vacation. We went to New York by car. It was only 200 miles, so we got there in one afternoon. The first day, we went to see the Statue of Liberty and the Empire State Building. My sister and I climbed to the top of the Statue of Liberty. That was a lot of fun!

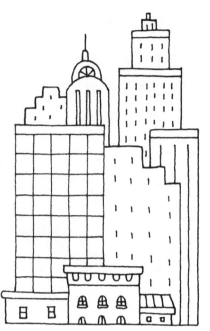

1. How did the family get to New York?

   ◯ By car.

   ◯ By bus.

   ◯ By train.

2. How many miles was the trip?

   ◯ 100 miles.

   ◯ 200 miles.

   ◯ 50 miles.

3. What did they see?

   ◯ The World Trade Center.

   ◯ The Statue of Liberty.

   ◯ The Staten Island Ferry.

4. Who climbed to the top of the Statue of Liberty?

   ◯ Tina and her Mom.

   ◯ Tina and her Dad.

   ◯ Tina and her sister.

(Supports Language Activities Big Book B, Activity 36) **Identifying details.** Students read the paragraph silently, then answer the questions by marking the oval next to the correct answer. Then a volunteer reads the story aloud and other students answer the questions.

Look at the picture.
Write the missing word in the sentence.

1. fry

2. row

3. climb

4. hurry

5. dry

6. play

This is what a father and his son and daughter
did last weekend. They camped near a big pond.

1. The father _____fried_____ eggs for breakfast.

2. In the afternoon, they _____ to an island.

3. They _____ a mountain. It started to rain.

4. They _____ back to their tent.

5. They _____ off inside the tent.

6. They _____ some games.

(Supports Language Activities Big Book B, Activity 37) **Constructing simple past tense; completing sentences.** Students complete the story by looking at the illustration that goes with each sentence and writing the past tense of the given verb on the line provided. Encourage students to read the completed story to a partner and ask and answer questions about the pictures. As sentences are read aloud, stress the -d end sound of these past tense verbs.

The Ungrateful Tiger

Choose a character from the story.
Write the character's name in the middle of the page.
Answer the questions about your character.

Where does your character live?

How does your character look? Draw a picture.

_____
character's name

What other adventures could your character have?

What problems does your character have?

© Addison-Wesley Publishing Company

(Supports Student Book B, pages 72-76) **Understanding character traits, identifying story setting, extending story ideas.** Students recall the characters in the play, and choose one character to feature on their page. Review the directions with the students. Students can write and or draw their answers. Encourage students to share and discuss their completed page.

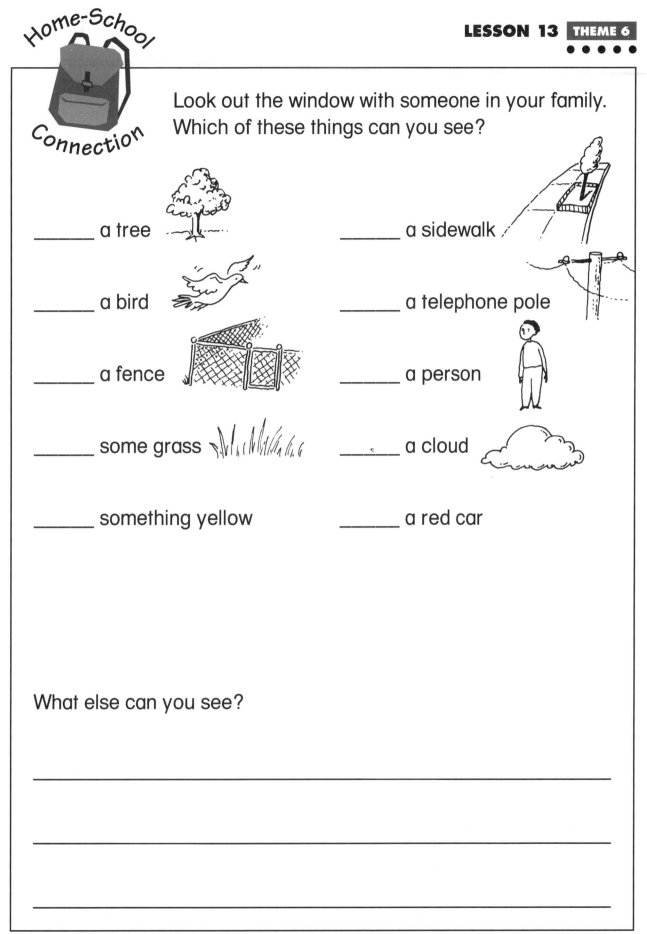

Look out the window with someone in your family. Which of these things can you see?

_____ a tree

_____ a bird

_____ a fence

_____ some grass

_____ something yellow

_____ a sidewalk

_____ a telephone pole

_____ a person

_____ a cloud

_____ a red car

What else can you see?

_____

_____

_____

(Supports Big Book: *Here It's Winter*) **Home-School Connection.** Review the directions with the students. Students take this page home to complete with a family member. Ask them to bring the page back to school to share and discuss with their classmates.

103

Data Collection

Grow some salad sprouts to eat.
Start with two different types of seeds.
Look at the seeds every day.
Draw pictures on the charts below.

Seeds #1 _____

1st day   2nd day   3rd day   4th day   5th day

These seeds sprouted in _____ days.

Seeds #2 _____

1st day   2nd day   3rd day   4th day   5th day

These seeds sprouted in _____ days.

Eat the sprouts with cream cheese or peanut butter on a cracker.

Which sprouts do you like best? _____

(Supports Student Book B, page 77) **Recording observations; comparing and contrasting; making predictions.** The Teacher's Guide provides simple suggestions for obtaining alfalfa and mung bean seeds, making or buying a sprouting jar, and growing the sprouts. The sprouts will be ready to eat in 4-5 days. Have students observe the sprouts daily and draw their observations — they may enjoy using magnifiers. Encourage them to compare and contrast the two seeds and make predictions.

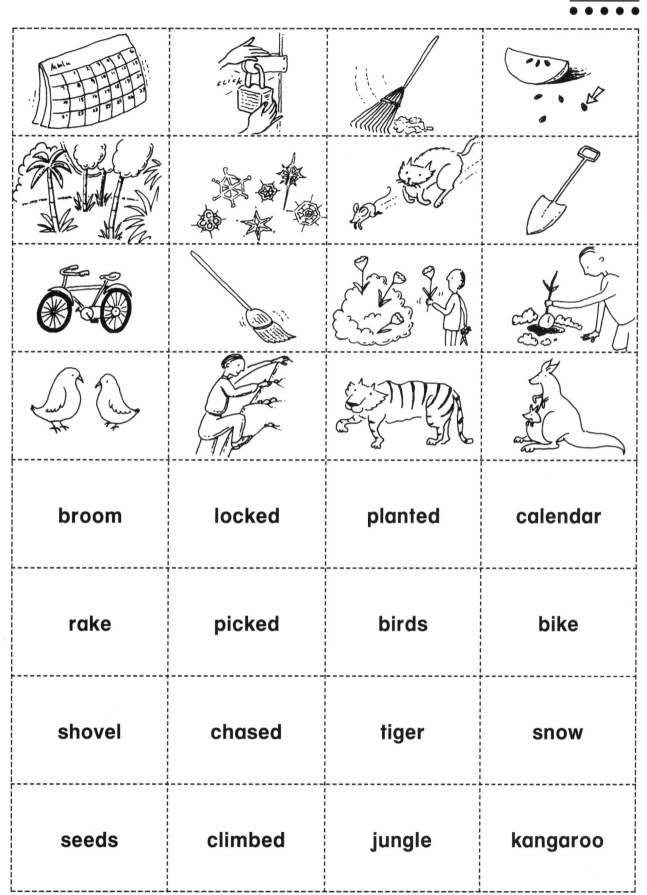

broom	locked	planted	calendar
rake	picked	birds	bike
shovel	chased	tiger	snow
seeds	climbed	jungle	kangaroo

Reinforcing key vocabulary. Have students cut out the cards and match pictures with words. Students can use the set of cards (16 picture cards and 16 word cards) to play a game of Concentration alone or with a partner. As a variation, two students may combine their picture cards, or their word cards and lay out a Concentration game in which they will hunt for picture or word pairs. The picture and word cards on this page will also be used with the Amazing Words game board on page 107.

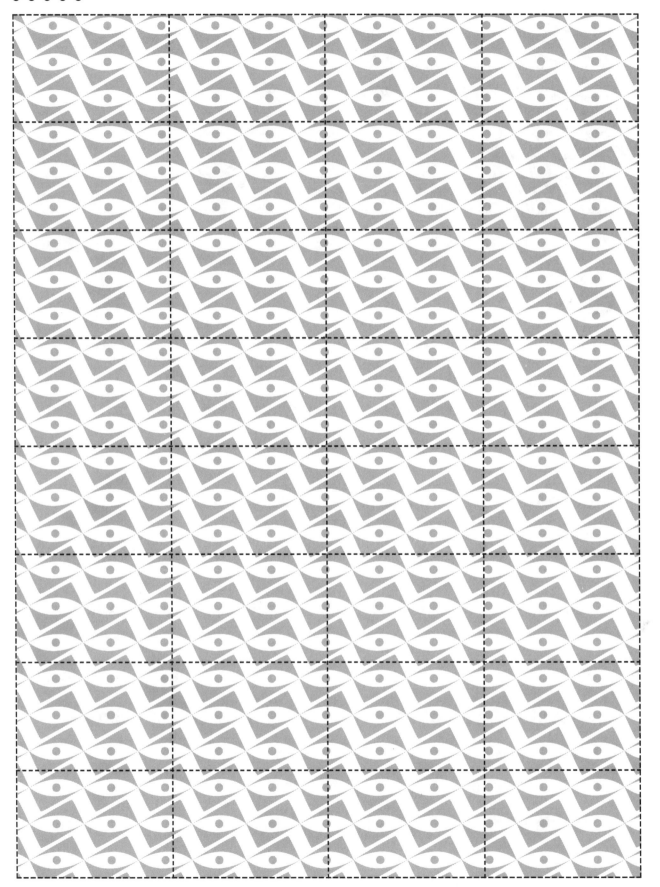

AMAZING WORDS

Put nine pictures on the game board.
Play an Amazing Words game.

Reinforcing key vocabulary. Each student chooses nine **picture cards** (provided on page 105) to glue on the game board. Two or three students play *Amazing Words* together. Players combine their sets of **word cards** from page 105 and place them face down on a table. In turn, each player picks up a word card and reads it aloud. If the matching picture appears on that player's game board, he or she places the word card on top of the picture. If not, the word card is returned to the table. The first player to fill his or her game board wins.

Vote for your favorite stories.
Put a star ★ in front of the three stories you like best.

☐ Hello Amigos (pages 4-7)

☐ The Tree Boy (pages 18-20)

☐ Tangram Tales (pages 21-23)

☐ Terrific Tarah (pages 30-32)

☐ The Knee-High Man (pages 34-38)

☐ A is for Astronaut (pages 44-46)

☐ Presents for America (pages 48-51)

☐ Why Rabbits Have Short Tails (pages 56-60)

☐ Busy Beavers (pages 62-64)

☐ The Ungrateful Tiger (pages 72-76)

Share your answers with your classmates. Talk about why you liked the stories. Which story did the whole class like best?

Student self-evaluation and reflection. Students express and share opinions about the stories they liked best. You may want to invite students to review the contents of this Skills Journal and/or their portfolio and choose the work they consider their best. Ask them to tell why they are proud of this work. You may want to use this page as a springboard for individual student conferences.